The Great Debate

The Great Debate: General Ability and Specific Abilities in the Prediction of Important Outcomes

Special Issue Editors

Harrison J. Kell
Jonas W.B. Lang

MDPI • Basel • Beijing • Wuhan • Barcelona • Belgrade

MDPI

Special Issue Editors
Harrison J. Kell
Educational Testing Service
USA

Jonas W.B. Lang
Ghent University
Belgium

Editorial Office
MDPI
St. Alban-Anlage 66
4052 Basel, Switzerland

This is a reprint of articles from the Special Issue published online in the open access journal *Journal of Intelligence* (ISSN 2079-3200) from 2018 to 2019 (available at: https://www.mdpi.com/journal/jintelligence/special_issues/great_debate).

For citation purposes, cite each article independently as indicated on the article page online and as indicated below:

LastName, A.A.; LastName, B.B.; LastName, C.C. Article Title. *Journal Name* **Year**, *Article Number*, Page Range.

ISBN 978-3-03921-167-8 (Pbk)
ISBN 978-3-03921-168-5 (PDF)

Cover image courtesy of unsplash.com

Contents

About the Special Issue Editors

Harrison J. Kell received his A.B. in psychology from Vassar College and his Ph.D. in industrial/organizational psychology from Rice University. He completed a postdoctoral fellowship in the Quantitative Methods program at Peabody College, Vanderbilt University. Currently, he is a Research Scientist in the Academic to Career Research Center at Educational Testing Service (ETS), located in Princeton, New Jersey, in the United States. He received the Award for Research Excellence from the Mensa Education and Research Foundation in both 2015 and 2016.

Jonas W.B. Lang received his psychology degree from the University of Mannheim and his Ph.D. from RWTH Aachen University in Germany. He previously was a lecturer at Maastricht University in the Netherlands. Currently, he is an Associate Professor in the Department of Personnel Management, Work, and Organizational Psychology at Ghent University in Ghent, Belgium. Jonas currently serves as an Associate Editor for *Organizational Research Methods* and the *Journal of Personnel Psychology* and is an editorial board member for a number of journals including the *Journal of Applied Psychology* and *Psychological Assessment*. He received the 2019 Jeanneret Award for Excellence in the Study of Individual or Group Assessment from the Society of Industrial and Organizational Psychology.

Preface to "The Great Debate: General Ability and Specific Abilities in the Prediction of Important Outcomes"

The structure of intelligence has been of interest to researchers and practitioners for over a century. Throughout much of the history of this research, there has been disagreement about how best to conceptualize the interrelations of general and specific cognitive abilities. Although this disagreement has largely been resolved through the integration of specific and general abilities via hierarchical models, there remain strong differences of opinion about the usefulness of abilities of differing breadth for predicting meaningful real-world outcomes. Paralleling inquiry into the structure of cognitive abilities, this "great debate" about the relative practical utility of measures of specific and general abilities has also existed nearly as long as scientific inquiry into intelligence itself. The papers collected in this volume inform and extend this important conversation.

Harrison J. Kell, Jonas W.B. Lang
Special Issue Editors

Journal of
Intelligence

MDPI

Editorial

The Great Debate: General Ability and Specific Abilities in the Prediction of Important Outcomes

Harrison J. Kell [1,*] and Jonas W. B. Lang [2,*]

[1]   Academic to Career Research Center, Research & Development, Educational Testing Service, Princeton, NJ 08541, USA
[2]   Department of Personnel Management, Work, and Organizational Psychology, Ghent University, Henri Dunantlaan 2, 9000 Ghent, Belgium
*   Correspondence: hkell@ets.org (H.J.K.); Jonas.Lang@UGent.be (J.W.B.L.); Tel.: +1-609-252-8511 (H.J.K.)

Received: 15 May 2018; Accepted: 28 May 2018; Published: 7 September 2018

Abstract: The relative value of specific versus general cognitive abilities for the prediction of practical outcomes has been debated since the inception of modern intelligence theorizing and testing. This editorial introduces a special issue dedicated to exploring this ongoing "great debate". It provides an overview of the debate, explains the motivation for the special issue and two types of submissions solicited, and briefly illustrates how differing conceptualizations of cognitive abilities demand different analytic strategies for predicting criteria, and that these different strategies can yield conflicting findings about the real-world importance of general versus specific abilities.

Keywords: bifactor model; cognitive abilities; educational attainment; general mental ability; hierarchical factor model; higher-order factor model; intelligence; job performance; nested-factors model; relative importance analysis; specific abilities

1. Introduction to the Special Issue

"To state one argument is not necessarily to be deaf to all others."

—Robert Louis Stevenson [1] (p. 11).

Measuring intelligence with the express purpose of predicting practical outcomes has played a major role in the discipline since its exception [2]. The apparent failure of sensory tests of intelligence to predict school grades led to their demise [3,4]. The Binet-Simon [5] was created with the practical goal of identifying students with developmental delays in order to track them into different schools as universal public education was instituted in France [6]. The Binet-Simon is considered the first "modern" intelligence test because it succeeded in fulfilling its purpose and, in doing so, served as a model for all the tests that followed it. Hugo Munsterberg, a pioneer of industrial/organizational psychology [7], used, and advocated the use of, intelligence tests for personnel selection [8–10]. Historically, intelligence testing comprised a major branch of applied psychology due to it being widely practiced in schools, the workplace and the military [11–14], as it is today [15–18].

For as long as psychometric tests have been used to chart the basic structure of intelligence and predict criteria outside the laboratory (e.g., grades, job performance), there has been tension between emphasizing general and specific abilities [19–21]. Insofar as the basic structure of individual differences in cognitive abilities, these tensions have largely been resolved by integrating specific and general abilities into hierarchical models. In the applied realm, however, debate remains.

This state of affairs may seem surprising, as from the 1980s to the early 2000s, research findings consistently demonstrated that specific abilities were relatively useless for predicting important real-world outcomes (e.g., grades, job performance) once *g* was accounted for [22]. This point of view is perhaps best characterized by the moniker "Not Much More Than *g*" (NMM*g*) [23–26]. Nonetheless, even during the high-water mark of this point of view, there were occasional dissenters who explicitly questioned it [27–29] or conducted research demonstrating that sometimes specific abilities *did* account for useful incremental validity beyond *g* [30–33]. Furthermore, when surveys explicitly asked about the relative value of general and specific abilities for applied prediction, substantial disagreement was revealed [34,35]. Since the apogee of NMM*g*, there has been a growing revival of using specific abilities to predict applied criteria (e.g., [20,36–49]). Recently, there have been calls to investigate the applied potential of specific abilities (e.g., [50–57]), and personnel selection researchers are actively reexamining whether specific abilities have value beyond *g* for predicting performance [58]. The research literature supporting NMM*g* cannot be denied, however, and the point of view it represents retains its allure for interpreting many practical findings (e.g., [59,60]). The purpose of this special issue is to continue the "great debate" about the relative practical value of measures of specific and general abilities.

We solicited two types of contributions for the special issue. The first type of invitation was for nonempirical theoretical, critical or integrative perspectives on the issue of general versus specific abilities for predicting real-world outcomes. The second type was empirical and inspired by Bliese, Halverson and Schriesheim's [61] approach: We provided a covariance matrix and the raw data for three intelligence measures from a Thurstonian test battery and school grades in a sample of German adolescents. Contributors were invited to analyze the data as they saw fit, with the overarching purpose of addressing three major questions:

- Do the data present evidence for the usefulness of specific abilities?
- How important are specific abilities relative to general abilities for predicting grades?
- To what degree could (or should) researchers use different prediction models for each of the different outcome criteria?

In asking contributors to analyze the same data according to their own theoretical and practical viewpoint(s), we hoped to draw out assumptions and perspectives that might otherwise remain implicit.

2. Data Provided

We provided a covariance matrix of the relationships between scores on three intelligence tests from a Thurstonian test battery and school grades in a sample of 219 German adolescents and young adults who were enrolled in a German middle, high or vocational school. The data were gathered directly at the schools or at a local fair for young adults interested in vocational education. A portion of these data were the basis for analyses published in Lang and Lang [62].

The intelligence tests came from the Wilde Intelligence test—a test rooted in Thurstone's work in the 1940s that was developed in Germany in the 1950s with the original purpose of selecting civil service employees; the test is widely used in Europe due to its long history, and is now available in a revised version. The most recent iteration of this battery [63] includes a recommendation for a short form that consists of the three tests that generated the scores included in our data. The first test ("unfolding") measures figural reasoning, the second consists of a relatively complex number-series task (and thus also measures reasoning), and third comprises verbal analogies. All three tests are speeded, meaning missingness is somewhat related to performance on the tests.

Grades in Germany are commonly rated on a scale ranging from very good (6) to poor (1). Poor is rarely used in the system and sometimes combined with insufficient (2), and thus rarely appears in the data supplied. The scale is roughly equivalent to the American grading system of A to F. The data include participants' sex, age, and grades in Math, German, English and Sports.

We originally provided the data as a covariance matrix and aggregated raw data file but also shared item data with interested authors. We view them as fairly typical of intelligence data gathered in school and other applied settings.

3. Theoretical Motivation

We judged it particularly important to draw out contributors' theoretical and practical assumptions because different conceptualizations of intelligence require different approaches to data analysis in order to appropriately model the relations between abilities and criteria. Alternatives to models of intelligence rooted in Spearman's original theory have existed almost since the inception of that theory (e.g., [64–68]), but have arisen with seemingly increasing regularity in the last 15 years (e.g., [69–74]). Unlike some other alternatives (e.g., [75–79]), most of these models do not cast doubt on the very existence of a general psychometric factor, but they do differ in its interpretation. These theories intrinsically offer differing outlooks on how g relates to specific abilities and, by extension, how to model relationships among g, specific abilities and practical outcomes. We illustrate this point by briefly outlining how the two hierarchical factor-analytic models most widely used for studying abilities at different strata [73] demand different analytic strategies to appropriately examine how those abilities relate to external criteria.

The first type of hierarchical conceptualization is the higher-order (HO) model. In this family of models, the pervasive positive intercorrelations among scores on tests of specific abilities are taken to imply a "higher-order" latent trait that accounts for them. Although HO models (e.g., [80,81]) differ in the number and composition of their ability strata, they ultimately posit a general factor that sits atop their hierarchies. Thus, although HO models acknowledge the existence of specific abilities, they also treat g as a construct that accounts for much of the variance in those abilities and, by extension, whatever outcomes those narrower abilities are predictive of. By virtue of the fact that g resides at the apex of the specific ability hierarchies in these models, those abilities are ultimately "subordinate" to it [82].

A second family of hierarchical models consists of the bifactor or nested-factor (NF) models [30]. Typically, in this class of models a general latent factor associated with all observed variables is specified, along with narrower latent factors associated with only a subset of observed variables (see Reise [83] for more details). In the context of cognitive abilities assessment, this general latent factor is usually treated as representing g, and the narrower factors interpreted as representing specific abilities, depending upon the content of the test battery and the data analytic procedures implemented (e.g., [84]). As a consequence, g and specific ability factors are treated as uncorrelated in NF models. Unlike in HO models, these factors are not conceptualized as existing at different "levels", but instead are treated as differing along a continuum of generality. In the NF family of models, the defining characteristic of the abilities is breadth, rather than subordination [82].

Lang et al. [20] illustrated that whether an HO or NF model is chosen to conceptualize individual differences in intelligence has important implications for analyzing the proportional relevance of general and specific abilities for predicting outcomes. When an HO model is selected, variance that is shared among g, specific abilities and a criterion will be attributed to g, as g is treated as a latent construct that accounts for variance in those specific abilities. As a consequence, only variance that is not shared between g and specific abilities is treated as a unique predictor of the criterion. This state of affairs is depicted in terms of predicting job performance with g and a single specific ability in panels A and B of Figure 1. In these scenarios, a commonly adopted approach is hierarchical regression, with g scores entered in the first step and specific ability scores in the second. In these situations, specific abilities typically account for a small amount of variance in the criterion beyond g [19,20].

When an NF model is selected to conceptualize individual differences in intelligence, g and specific abilities are treated as uncorrelated, necessitating a different analytic strategy than the traditional incremental validity approach when predicting practical criteria. Depending on the composition of the test(s) being used, some data analytic approaches include explicitly using a bifactor method to estimate g and specific abilities, and predicting criteria using the resultant latent variables [33], extracting g from test scores first and then using the residuals representing specific abilities to predict criteria [37], or using relative-importance analyses to ensure that variance shared among g, specific abilities and the criterion is not automatically attributed to g [20,44,47]. This final strategy is depicted in panels C and D of Figure 1. When an NF perspective is adopted, and the analyses are properly aligned with it, results often show that specific abilities can account for substantial variance in criteria beyond g and are sometimes even more important predictors than g [19].

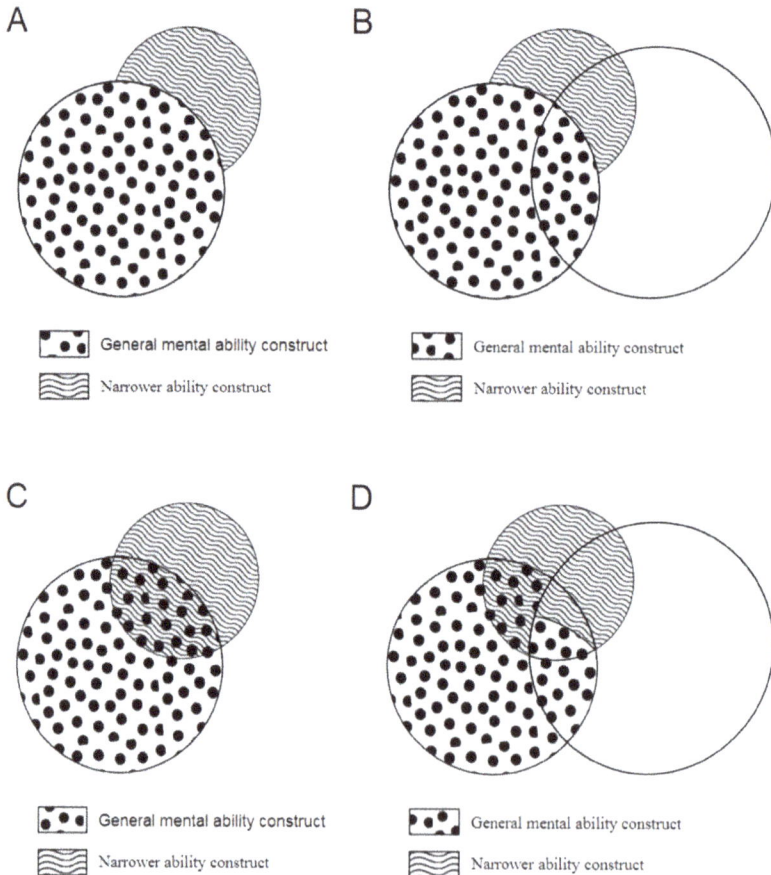

Figure 1. This figure depicts a simplified scenario with a single general mental ability (GMA) measure and a single narrow cognitive ability measure. As shown in Panel A, higher-order models attribute all shared variance between the GMA measure and the narrower cognitive ability measure to GMA. Panel B depicts the consequence of this type of conceptualization: Criterion variance in job performance jointly explained by the GMA measure and the narrower cognitive ability measure is solely attributed to GMA. Nested-factors models, in contrast, do not assume that the variance shared by the GMA measure and narrower cognitive ability measure is wholly attributable to GMA and distributes the variance across the two constructs (Panel C). Accordingly, as illustrated in Panel D, criterion variance in job performance jointly explained by the GMA measure and the narrower cognitive ability measure may be attributable to either the GMA construct or the narrower cognitive ability construct. Adapted from Lang et al. [20] (p. 599).

The HO and NF conceptualizations are in many ways only a starting point for thinking about how to model relations among abilities of differing generality and practical criteria. Other approaches in (or related to) the factor-analytic tradition that can be used to explore these associations include the hierarchies of factor solutions method [73,85], behavior domain theory [86], and formative measurement models [87]. Other treatments of intelligence that reside outside the factor analytic tradition (e.g., [88,89]) and treat *g* as an emergent phenomenon represent new challenges (and opportunities) for studying the relative importance of different strata of abilities for predicting practical outcomes. The existence of these many possibilities for modeling differences in human cognitive abilities underscores the need for researchers and practitioners to select their analytic techniques carefully, in order to ensure those techniques are properly aligned with the model of intelligence being invoked.

4. Editorial Note on the Contributions

The articles in this special issue were solicited from scholars who have demonstrated expertise in the investigation of not only human intelligence but also cognitive abilities of differing breadth and their associations with applied criteria. Consequently, we believe this collection of papers both provides an excellent overview of the ongoing debate about the relative practical importance of general and specific abilities, and substantially advances this debate. As editors, we have reviewed these contributions through multiple iterations of revision, and in all cases the authors were highly responsive to our feedback. We are proud to be the editors of a special issue that consists of such outstanding contributions to the field.

Author Contributions: H.J.K. and J.W.B.L. conceived the general scope of the editorial; H.J.K. primarily wrote Sections 1 and 4; J.W.B.L. primarily wrote Section 2; H.J.K. and J.W.B.L. contributed equally to Section 3; H.J.K. and J.W.B.L. reviewed and revised each other's respective sections.

Conflicts of Interest: The authors declare no conflict of interest.

References

1. Stevenson, R.L. *An Apology for Idlers and Other Essays*; Thomas B. Mosher: Portland, ME, USA, 1916.
2. Danziger, K. *Naming the Mind: How Psychology Found Its Language*; Sage: London, UK, 1997.
3. Sharp, S.E. Individual psychology: A study in psychological method. *Am. J. Psychol.* **1899**, *10*, 329–391. [CrossRef]
4. Wissler, C. The correlation of mental and physical tests. *Psychol. Rev.* **1901**, *3*, i-62. [CrossRef]
5. Binet, A.; Simon, T. New methods for the diagnosis of the intellectual level of subnormals. *L'Annee Psychol.* **1905**, *12*, 191–244.
6. Schneider, W.H. After Binet: French intelligence testing, 1900–1950. *J. Hist. Behav. Sci.* **1992**, *28*, 111–132. [CrossRef]
7. Benjamin, L.T. Hugo Münsterberg: Portrait of an applied psychologist. In *Portraits of Pioneers in Psychology*; Kimble, G.A., Wertheimer, M., Eds.; Erlbaum: Mahwah, NJ, USA, 2000; Volume 4, pp. 113–129.
8. Kell, H.J.; Lubinski, D. Spatial ability: A neglected talent in educational and occupational settings. *Roeper Rev.* **2013**, *35*, 219–230. [CrossRef]
9. Kevles, D.J. Testing the Army's intelligence: Psychologists and the military in World War I. *J. Am. Hist.* **1968**, *55*, 565–581. [CrossRef]
10. Moskowitz, M.J. Hugo Münsterberg: A study in the history of applied psychology. *Am. Psychol.* **1977**, *32*, 824–842. [CrossRef]
11. Bingham, W.V. On the possibility of an applied psychology. *Psychol. Rev.* **1923**, *30*, 289–305. [CrossRef]
12. Katzell, R.A.; Austin, J.T. From then to now: The development of industrial-organizational psychology in the United States. *J. Appl. Psychol.* **1992**, *77*, 803–835. [CrossRef]
13. Sackett, P.R.; Lievens, F.; Van Iddekinge, C.H.; Kuncel, N.R. Individual differences and their measurement: A review of 100 years of research. *J. Appl. Psychol.* **2017**, *102*, 254–273. [CrossRef] [PubMed]
14. Terman, L.M. The status of applied psychology in the United States. *J. Appl. Psychol.* **1921**, *5*, 1–4. [CrossRef]
15. Gardner, H. Who owns intelligence? *Atl. Mon.* **1999**, *283*, 67–76.
16. Gardner, H.E. *Intelligence Reframed: Multiple Intelligences for the 21st Century*; Hachette UK: London, UK, 2000.
17. Sternberg, R.J. (Ed.) North American approaches to intelligence. In *International Handbook of Intelligence*; Cambridge University Press: Cambridge, UK, 2004; pp. 411–444.
18. Sternberg, R.J. Testing: For better and worse. *Phi Delta Kappan* **2016**, *98*, 66–71. [CrossRef]

19. Kell, H.J.; Lang, J.W.B. Specific abilities in the workplace: More important than *g*? *J. Intell.* **2017**, *5*, 13. [CrossRef]
20. Lang, J.W.B.; Kersting, M.; Hülsheger, U.R.; Lang, J. General mental ability, narrower cognitive abilities, and job performance: The perspective of the nested-factors model of cognitive abilities. *Pers. Psychol.* **2010**, *63*, 595–640. [CrossRef]
21. Thorndike, R.M.; Lohman, D.F. *A Century of Ability Testing*; Riverside: Chicago, IL, USA, 1990.
22. Murphy, K. What can we learn from "Not Much More than *g*"? *J. Intell.* **2017**, *5*, 8. [CrossRef]
23. Olea, M.M.; Ree, M.J. Predicting pilot and navigator criteria: Not much more than *g*. *J. Appl. Psychol.* **1994**, *79*, 845–851. [CrossRef]
24. Ree, M.J.; Earles, J.A. Predicting training success: Not much more than *g*. *Pers. Psychol.* **1991**, *44*, 321–332. [CrossRef]
25. Ree, M.J.; Earles, J.A. Predicting occupational criteria: Not much more than *g*. In *Human Abilities: Their Nature and Measurement*; Dennis, I., Tapsfield, P., Eds.; Erlbaum: Mahwah, NJ, USA, 1996; pp. 151–165.
26. Ree, M.J.; Earles, J.A.; Teachout, M.S. Predicting job performance: Not much more than *g*. *J. Appl. Psychol.* **1994**, *79*, 518–524. [CrossRef]
27. Bowman, D.B.; Markham, P.M.; Roberts, R.D. Expanding the frontier of human cognitive abilities: So much more than (plain) *g*! *Learn. Individ. Differ.* **2002**, *13*, 127–158. [CrossRef]
28. Murphy, K.R. Individual differences and behavior in organizations: Much more than *g*. In *Individual Differences and Behavior in Organizations*; Murphy, K., Ed.; Jossey-Bass: San Francisco, CA, USA, 1996; pp. 3–30.
29. Stankov, L. *g*: A diminutive general. In *The General Factor of Intelligence: How General Is It?* Sternberg, R.J., Grigorenko, E.L., Eds.; Erlbaum: Mahwah, NJ, USA, 2002; pp. 19–37.
30. Gustafsson, J.-E.; Balke, G. General and specific abilities as predictors of school achievement. *Multivar. Behav. Res.* **1993**, *28*, 407–434. [CrossRef] [PubMed]
31. LePine, J.A.; Hollenbeck, J.R.; Ilgen, D.R.; Hedlund, J. Effects of individual differences on the performance of hierarchical decision-making teams: Much more than *g*. *J. Appl. Psychol.* **1997**, *82*, 803–811. [CrossRef]
32. Levine, E.L.; Spector, P.E.; Menon, S.; Narayanan, L. Validity generalization for cognitive, psychomotor, and perceptual tests for craft jobs in the utility industry. *Hum. Perform.* **1996**, *9*, 1–22. [CrossRef]
33. Reeve, C.L. Differential ability antecedents of general and specific dimensions of declarative knowledge: More than *g*. *Intelligence* **2004**, *32*, 621–652. [CrossRef]
34. Murphy, K.R.; Cronin, B.E.; Tam, A.P. Controversy and consensus regarding the use of cognitive ability testing in organizations. *J. Appl. Psychol.* **2003**, *88*, 660–671. [CrossRef] [PubMed]
35. Reeve, C.L.; Charles, J.E. Survey of opinions on the primacy of *g* and social consequences of ability testing: A comparison of expert and non-expert views. *Intelligence* **2008**, *36*, 681–688. [CrossRef]
36. Coyle, T.R. Ability tilt for whites and blacks: Support for differentiation and investment theories. *Intelligence* **2016**, *56*, 28–34. [CrossRef]
37. Coyle, T.R. Non-*g* residuals of group factors predict ability tilt, college majors, and jobs: A non-*g* nexus. *Intelligence* **2018**, *67*, 19–25. [CrossRef]
38. Coyle, T.R.; Pillow, D.R. SAT and ACT predict college GPA after removing *g*. *Intelligence* **2008**, *36*, 719–729. [CrossRef]
39. Coyle, T.R.; Purcell, J.M.; Snyder, A.C.; Richmond, M.C. Ability tilt on the SAT and ACT predicts specific abilities and college majors. *Intelligence* **2014**, *46*, 18–24. [CrossRef]
40. Coyle, T.R.; Snyder, A.C.; Richmond, M.C. Sex differences in ability tilt: Support for investment theory. *Intelligence* **2015**, *50*, 209–220. [CrossRef]
41. Coyle, T.R.; Snyder, A.C.; Richmond, M.C.; Little, M. SAT non-*g* residuals predict course specific GPAs: Support for investment theory. *Intelligence* **2015**, *51*, 57–66. [CrossRef]
42. Kell, H.J.; Lubinski, D.; Benbow, C.P. Who rises to the top? Early indicators. *Psychol. Sci.* **2013**, *24*, 648–659. [CrossRef] [PubMed]
43. Kell, H.J.; Lubinski, D.; Benbow, C.P.; Steiger, J.H. Creativity and technical innovation: Spatial ability's unique role. *Psychol. Sci.* **2013**, *24*, 1831–1836. [CrossRef] [PubMed]
44. Lang, J.W.B.; Bliese, P.D. I–O psychology and progressive research programs on intelligence. *Ind. Organ. Psychol.* **2012**, *5*, 161–166. [CrossRef]

45. Makel, M.C.; Kell, H.J.; Lubinski, D.; Putallaz, M.; Benbow, C.P. When lightning strikes twice: Profoundly gifted, profoundly accomplished. *Psychol. Sci.* **2016**, *27*, 1004–1018. [CrossRef] [PubMed]

46. Park, G.; Lubinski, D.; Benbow, C.P. Contrasting intellectual patterns predict creativity in the arts and sciences: Tracking intellectually precocious youth over 25 years. *Psychol. Sci.* **2007**, *18*, 948–952. [CrossRef] [PubMed]

47. Stanhope, D.S.; Surface, E.A. Examining the incremental validity and relative importance of specific cognitive abilities in a training context. *J. Pers. Psychol.* **2014**, *13*, 146–156. [CrossRef]

48. Wai, J.; Lubinski, D.; Benbow, C.P. Spatial ability for STEM domains: Aligning over 50 years of cumulative psychological knowledge solidifies its importance. *J. Educ. Psychol.* **2009**, *101*, 817–835. [CrossRef]

49. Ziegler, M.; Dietl, E.; Danay, E.; Vogel, M.; Bühner, M. Predicting training success with general mental ability, specific ability tests, and (Un) structured interviews: A meta-analysis with unique samples. *Int. J. Sel. Assess.* **2011**, *19*, 170–182. [CrossRef]

50. Lievens, F.; Reeve, C.L. Where I–O psychology should really (re)start its investigation of intelligence constructs and their measurement. *Ind. Organ. Psychol.* **2012**, *5*, 153–158. [CrossRef]

51. Coyle, T.R. Predictive validity of non-*g* residuals of tests: More than *g*. *J. Intell.* **2014**, *2*, 21–25. [CrossRef]

52. Flynn, J.R. Reflections about Intelligence over 40 Years. *Intelligence* **2018**. Available online: https://www.sciencedirect.com/science/article/pii/S0160289618300904?dgcid=raven_sd_aip_email (accessed on 31 August 2018).

53. Reeve, C.L.; Scherbaum, C.; Goldstein, H. Manifestations of intelligence: Expanding the measurement space to reconsider specific cognitive abilities. *Hum. Resour. Manag. Rev.* **2015**, *25*, 28–37. [CrossRef]

54. Ritchie, S.J.; Bates, T.C.; Deary, I.J. Is education associated with improvements in general cognitive ability, or in specific skills? *Devel. Psychol.* **2015**, *51*, 573–582. [CrossRef] [PubMed]

55. Schneider, W.J.; Newman, D.A. Intelligence is multidimensional: Theoretical review and implications of specific cognitive abilities. *Hum. Resour. Manag. Rev.* **2015**, *25*, 12–27. [CrossRef]

56. Krumm, S.; Schmidt-Atzert, L.; Lipnevich, A.A. Insights beyond *g*: Specific cognitive abilities at work. *J. Pers. Psychol.* **2014**, *13*, 117–122. [CrossRef]

57. Wee, S.; Newman, D.A.; Song, Q.C. More than g-factors: Second-stratum factors should not be ignored. *Ind. Organ. Psychol.* **2015**, *8*, 482–488. [CrossRef]

58. Ryan, A.M.; Ployhart, R.E. A century of selection. *Annu. Rev. Psychol.* **2014**, *65*, 693–717. [CrossRef] [PubMed]

59. Gottfredson, L.S. A *g* theorist on why Kovacs and Conway's Process Overlap Theory amplifies, not opposes, *g* theory. *Psychol. Inq.* **2016**, *27*, 210–217. [CrossRef]

60. Ree, M.J.; Carretta, T.R.; Teachout, M.S. Pervasiveness of dominant general factors in organizational measurement. *Ind. Organ. Psychol.* **2015**, *8*, 409–427. [CrossRef]

61. Bliese, P.D.; Halverson, R.R.; Schriesheim, C.A. Benchmarking multilevel methods in leadership: The articles, the model, and the data set. *Leadersh. Quart.* **2002**, *13*, 3–14. [CrossRef]

62. Lang, J.W.B.; Lang, J. Priming competence diminishes the link between cognitive test anxiety and test performance: Implications for the interpretation of test scores. *Psychol. Sci.* **2010**, *21*, 811–819. [CrossRef] [PubMed]

63. Kersting, M.; Althoff, K.; Jäger, A.O. *Wilde-Intelligenz-Test 2: WIT-2*; Hogrefe, Verlag für Psychologie: Göttingen, Germany, 2008.

64. Brown, W. Some experimental results in the correlation of mental abilities. *Br. J. Psychol.* **1910**, *3*, 296–322.

65. Brown, W.; Thomson, G.H. *The Essentials of Mental Measurement*; Cambridge University Press: Cambridge, UK, 1921.

66. Thorndike, E.L.; Lay, W.; Dean, P.R. The relation of accuracy in sensory discrimination to general intelligence. *Am. J. Psychol.* **1909**, *20*, 364–369. [CrossRef]

67. Tryon, R.C. A theory of psychological components—An alternative to "mathematical factors". *Psychol. Rev.* **1935**, *42*, 425–445. [CrossRef]

68. Tryon, R.C. Reliability and behavior domain validity: Reformulation and historical critique. *Psychol. Bull.* **1957**, *54*, 229–249. [CrossRef] [PubMed]

69. Bartholomew, D.J.; Allerhand, M.; Deary, I.J. Measuring mental capacity: Thomson's Bonds model and Spearman's *g*-model compared. *Intelligence* **2013**, *41*, 222–233. [CrossRef]

70. Dickens, W.T. What Is *g*? Available online: https://www.brookings.edu/wp-content/uploads/2016/06/20070503.pdf (accessed on 2 May 2018).

71. Kievit, R.A.; Davis, S.W.; Griffiths, J.; Correia, M.M.; Henson, R.N. A watershed model of individual differences in fluid intelligence. *Neuropsychologia* **2016**, *91*, 186–198. [CrossRef] [PubMed]

72. Kovacs, K.; Conway, A.R. Process overlap theory: A unified account of the general factor of intelligence. *Psychol. Inq.* **2016**, *27*, 151–177. [CrossRef]

73. Lang, J.W.B.; Kersting, M.; Beauducel, A. Hierarchies of factor solutions in the intelligence domain: Applying methodology from personality psychology to gain insights into the nature of intelligence. *Learn. Individ. Differ.* **2016**, *47*, 37–50. [CrossRef]

74. Van Der Maas, H.L.; Dolan, C.V.; Grasman, R.P.; Wicherts, J.M.; Huizenga, H.M.; Raijmakers, M.E. A dynamical model of general intelligence: The positive manifold of intelligence by mutualism. *Psychol. Rev.* **2006**, *113*, 842–861. [CrossRef] [PubMed]

75. Campbell, D.T.; Fiske, D.W. Convergent and discriminant validation by the multitrait-multimethod matrix. *Psychol. Bull.* **1959**, *56*, 81–105. [CrossRef] [PubMed]

76. Gould, S.J. *The Mismeasure of Man*, 2nd ed.; W. W. Norton & Company: New York, NY, USA, 1996.

77. Howe, M.J. Separate skills or general intelligence: The autonomy of human abilities. *Br. J. Educ. Psychol.* **1989**, *59*, 351–360. [CrossRef]

78. Schlinger, H.D. The myth of intelligence. *Psychol. Record* **2003**, *53*, 15–32.

79. Schönemann, P.H. Jensen's *g*: Outmoded theories and unconquered frontiers. In *Arthur Jensen: Consensus and Controversy*; Modgil, S., Modgil, C., Eds.; The Falmer Press: New York, NY, USA, 1987; pp. 313–328.

80. Johnson, W.; Bouchard, T.J. The structure of human intelligence: It is verbal, perceptual, and image rotation (VPR), not fluid and crystallized. *Intelligence* **2005**, *33*, 393–416. [CrossRef]

81. McGrew, K.S. CHC theory and the human cognitive abilities project: Standing on the shoulders of the giants of psychometric intelligence research. *Intelligence* **2009**, *37*, 1–10. [CrossRef]

82. Humphreys, L.G. The primary mental ability. In *Intelligence and Learning*; Friedman, M.P., Das, J.R., O'Connor, N., Eds.; Plenum: New York, NY, USA, 1981; pp. 87–102.

83. Reise, S.P. The rediscovery of bifactor measurement models. *Multivar. Behav. Res.* **2012**, *47*, 667–696. [CrossRef] [PubMed]

84. Murray, A.L.; Johnson, W. The limitations of model fit in comparing the bi-factor versus higher-order models of human cognitive ability structure. *Intelligence* **2013**, *41*, 407–422. [CrossRef]

85. Goldberg, L.R. Doing it all bass-ackwards: The development of hierarchical factor structures from the top down. *J. Res. Personal.* **2006**, *40*, 347–358. [CrossRef]

86. McDonald, R.P. Behavior domains in theory and in practice. *Alta. J. Educ. Res.* **2003**, *49*, 212–230.

87. Bollen, K.; Lennox, R. Conventional wisdom on measurement: A structural equation perspective. *Psychol. Bull.* **1991**, *110*, 305–314. [CrossRef]

88. Kievit, R.A.; Lindenberger, U.; Goodyer, I.M.; Jones, P.B.; Fonagy, P.; Bullmore, E.T.; Dolan, R.J. Mutualistic coupling between vocabulary and reasoning supports cognitive development during late adolescence and early adulthood. *Psychol. Sci.* **2017**, *28*, 1419–1431. [CrossRef] [PubMed]

89. Van Der Maas, H.L.; Kan, K.J.; Marsman, M.; Stevenson, C.E. Network models for cognitive development and intelligence. *J. Intell.* **2017**, *5*, 16. [CrossRef]

Journal of
Intelligence

MDPI

Article

Bifactor Models for Predicting Criteria by General and Specific Factors: Problems of Nonidentifiability and Alternative Solutions

Michael Eid [1,*]**, Stefan Krumm** [1]**, Tobias Koch** [2] **and Julian Schulze** [1]

[1] Department of Education and Psychology, Freie Universität Berlin, Habelschwerdter Allee 45,
    14195 Berlin, Germany; stefan.krumm@fu-berlin.de (S.K.); julian.schulze@fu-berlin.de (J.S.)
[2] Methodology Center, Leuphana Universität Lüneburg, 21335 Lüneburg, Germany; tobias.koch@leuphana.de
*   Correspondence: michael.eid@fu-berlin.de; Tel.: +49-308-385-5611

Received: 21 March 2018; Accepted: 5 September 2018; Published: 7 September 2018

Abstract: The bifactor model is a widely applied model to analyze general and specific abilities. Extensions of bifactor models additionally include criterion variables. In such extended bifactor models, the general and specific factors can be correlated with criterion variables. Moreover, the influence of general and specific factors on criterion variables can be scrutinized in latent multiple regression models that are built on bifactor measurement models. This study employs an extended bifactor model to predict mathematics and English grades by three facets of intelligence (number series, verbal analogies, and unfolding). We show that, if the observed variables do not differ in their loadings, extended bifactor models are not identified and not applicable. Moreover, we reveal that standard errors of regression weights in extended bifactor models can be very large and, thus, lead to invalid conclusions. A formal proof of the nonidentification is presented. Subsequently, we suggest alternative approaches for predicting criterion variables by general and specific factors. In particular, we illustrate how (1) composite ability factors can be defined in extended first-order factor models and (2) how bifactor(*S*-1) models can be applied. The differences between first-order factor models and bifactor(*S*-1) models for predicting criterion variables are discussed in detail and illustrated with the empirical example.

Keywords: bifactor model; identification; bifactor(*S*-1) model; general factor; specific factors

1. Introduction

In 1904, Charles Spearman [1] published his groundbreaking article *"General intelligence objectively determined and measured"* that has been affecting intelligence research since then. In this paper Spearman stated that "all branches of intellectual activity have in common one fundamental function (or groups of functions), whereas the remaining or specific elements of the activity seem in every case to be wholly different from that in all the others" (p. 284). Given Spearman's distinction into general and specific cognitive abilities, one fundamental topic of intelligence research has been the question to which degree these general and specific facets are important for predicting real-world criteria (e.g., [2,3]; for an overview see [4]). In other words, is it sufficient to consider *g* alone or do the other specific factors (also sometimes referred to as narrower factors) contribute in an essential way?

Around the year 2000, there was a unanimously agreed answer to this question. Several authors concluded that specific abilities do not explain much variance beyond *g* (e.g., [5,6]). In the past decade, however, this consensus has shifted from "not much more than *g*" (see [7]) to the notion that there may be something more than *g* predicting real-world criteria. Reflecting this shift, Kell and Lang [4] summarize that "recent studies have variously demonstrated the importance of narrower abilities above and beyond *g*." (p. 11). However, this debate is far from settled [8].

An apparent issue in evaluating discrepant findings across studies is the statistical approach applied. Much of the earlier evidence was based on hierarchical regression analyses, in which *g* (the first unrotated principle component) was entered in the first and specific cognitive abilities in the second step (e.g., [6]). Other studies relied on relative importance analysis (e.g., [9]), mediation models, in which criteria are predicted by *g* which in turn is predicted by specific abilities (e.g., [10]), as well as meta-analytical procedures (e.g., [11,12]). There is another prominent approach to separate general from specific abilities: the bifactor model [13]. Although its introduction dates way back, the bifactor model is recently and increasingly applied in studies predicting criterion variables by general and specific factors, not only in the area of cognitive abilities and school performance measures (e.g., [14–24]), but also in different other areas of psychological research such as motivation and engagement (e.g., [25–27]), clinical psychology (e.g., [28–30]), organizational psychology (e.g., [31]), personality psychology (e.g., [32,33]), and media psychology (e.g., [34]). The multitude of recently published studies using the bifactor model shows that it has become a standard model for predicting criterion variables by general and specific components.

In the current study, we seek to contribute to the debate on general versus specific cognitive abilities as predictors of real-life criteria by taking a closer look at the bifactor model. We will describe the basic idea of the bifactor model and its applicability for predicting criterion variables. We will also apply it to the data set provided by the editors of this special issue. In particular, we will show that the bifactor model is not generally identified when the prediction of criterion variables comes into play and can be affected by estimation problems such as large standard errors of regression weights. To our knowledge, this insight has not been published previously. Subsequently, we will illustrate and discuss alternatives to the bifactor model. First, we will present a first-order factor model with correlated factors as well as an extension of this model, in which a composite intelligence factor is defined by the best linear combination of facets for predicting criterion variables. Second, we will discuss bifactor(*S*-1) models, which constitute recently developed alternatives to the bifactor approach [35]. We conclude that bifactor(*S*-1) models might be more appropriate for predicting criterion variables by general and specific factors in certain research areas.

Bifactor Model

The bifactor model was introduced by Holzinger and Swineford [13] to separate general from specific factors in the measurement of cognitive abilities. Although this model is quite old, it was seldom applied in the first seventy years of its existence. It has only become a standard for modeling *g*-factor structures in the last ten years [32,35–37]. When this model is applied to measure general and specific cognitive abilities, *g* is represented by a general factor that is common to all cognitive ability tests included in a study (see Figure 1a). In case of the three cognitive abilities considered in this study (number series, verbal analogies, and unfolding), the general factor represents variance that is shared by all three abilities. The cognitive ability tests additionally load on separate orthogonal factors—the specific factors. So, each specific factor, also sometimes referred to as group factor (e.g., [37]), represents a unique narrow ability. Because all factors in the classical bifactor model are assumed to be uncorrelated, the variance of an observed measure of cognitive abilities can be decomposed into three parts: (1) measurement error, (2) the general factor, and (3) the specific factors. This decomposition of variance allows estimating to which degree observed differences in cognitive abilities are determined by *g* or by the specific components.

The bifactor model is also considered a very attractive model for predicting criterion variables by general and specific factors (e.g., [32]). It becomes attractive for such purposes since the general and the specific factors—as specified in the bifactor model—are uncorrelated, thus representing unique variance that is not shared with the other factors. Hence, they contribute independently of each other to the prediction of the criterion variable. In other words, the regression coefficients in a multiple regression analysis (see Figure 1c) do not depend on the other factors in the model. Consequently, the explained criterion variance can be additively decomposed into components that are determined by each general and specific factor.

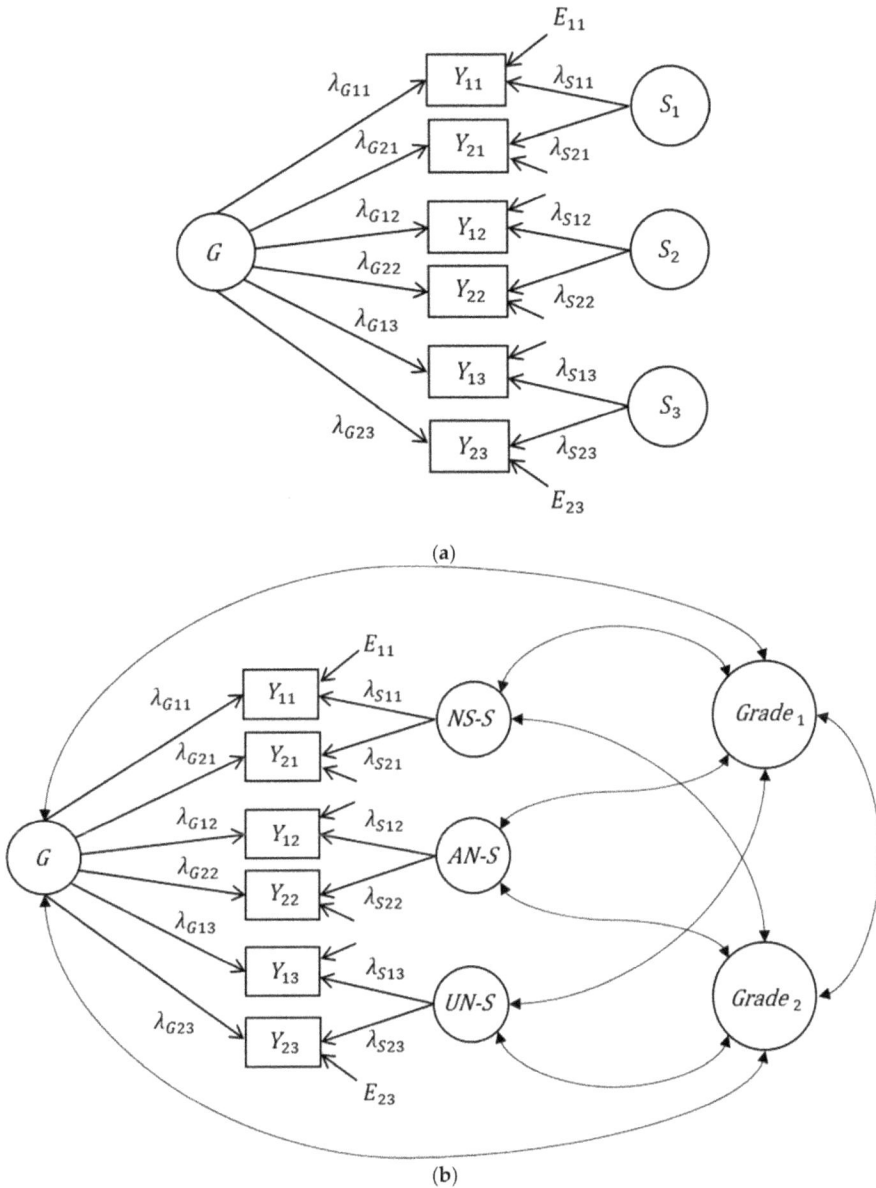

(a)

(b)

Figure 1. *Cont.*

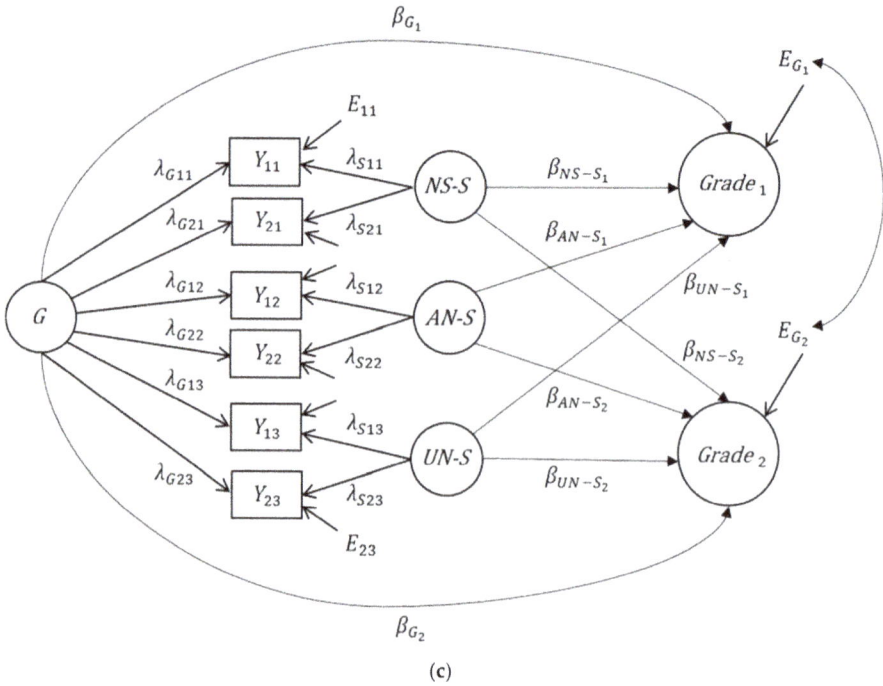

Figure 1. Bifactor model and its extensions to criterion variables. (**a**) Bifactor model without criterion variables, (**b**) bifactor model with correlating criterion variables (grades), and (**c**) multiple latent regression bifactor model. The factors of the extended models depicted refer to the empirical application. G: general factor, S_k: specific factors; *NS-S*: specific factor number series, *AN-S*: specific factor verbal analogies, *UN-S*: specific factor unfolding. E_{ik}: measurement error variables, E_{G1}/E_{G2}: residuals, λ: loading parameters, β: regression coefficients, i: indicator, k: facet.

On the one hand, these properties make the bifactor model very attractive for applied researchers. On the other hand, many studies that used bifactor models to predict criterion variables, hereinafter referred to as extended bifactor models (see Figure 1c), showed results that were not theoretically expected. For example, some of these studies revealed loadings (of indicators either on the *g* factor or on the specific factors) that were insignificant or even negative—although these items were theoretically assumed as indicators of these factors (e.g., [19,25,27–30]). Moreover, it was often observed that one of the specific factors was not necessary to predict criterion variables by general and specific factors (e.g., [14,18,19,32,33]). Similar results were often found in applications of non-extended versions of the bifactor model (see [35], for an extensive discussion of application problems of the bifactor model).

Beyond the unexpected results found in several studies that used bifactor models, its applicability is affected by a more fundamental problem. When a bifactor model is extended to criterion variables, the model is not globally identified—although the model without criterion variables is. As we will show below, the extended bifactor model is not applicable if the indicators do not differ in their loadings: it might be affected by estimation problems (e.g., large standard errors of regression coefficients) or even be unidentified. Next, we will use the data set provided by the editors of the special issue to illustrate this problem.

2. Description of the Empirical Study

2.1. Participants and Materials

We analyzed the data set provided by Kell and Lang [38]. It includes data from $n = 219$ individuals. Gender was almost equally distributed among the sample (53% female). Their mean age was 16 years ($SD = 1.49$, range = 13 to 23).

The data set included three subtests of the Wilde Intelligence Test 2 [39]. These subtests were: verbal analogies (complete a word pair so that it logically matches a given other word pair), number series (find the logical next number in a series of numbers), and figural unfolding (identify the 3-dimensional form that can be created by a given two-dimensional folding sheet). The number of correctly solved items within the time limit of each subtest serves as a participant's score. For the purpose of the current paper, we conducted an odd-even split of subtest items to obtain two indicators per each subtest. If achievement tests are split into two parts, an odd-even split is recommended for two main reasons. First, such tests usually contain a time limit. Hence, splitting tests in other ways would result in unbalanced parcels (one parcel would contain "later" items for which the time limit might have been more of a concern). Second, items are usually ordered so that item difficulty increases. Hence, the odd-even split ensures that items with approximately equal difficulty are assigned to both parcels.

We used two of the grades provided in the data set, mathematics and English. We chose these grades because we wanted to include a numerical and a verbal criterion. For more details about the data set and its collection, see Kell and Lang [38].

2.2. Data Analysis

The data was analyzed using the computer program Mplus Version 8 [40]. The observed intelligence test scores were taken as continuous variables whereas the grades were defined as categorical variables with ordered categories. The estimator used was the WLSMV estimator which is recommended for this type of analysis [40]. The correlations between the grades are polychoric correlations, the correlations between the grades and the intelligence variables are polyserial correlations whereas the correlations between the intelligence variables are Pearson correlations. The correlation matrix of the observed variables, on which the analyses are based, is given in Table 1. The correlations between test halves (created by an odd-even split) of the same intelligence facets were relatively large (between $r = 0.687$ and $r = 0.787$), thus showing that it is reasonable to consider the respective halves as indicators of the same latent intelligence factor. Correlations between grades and observed intelligence variables ranged from $r = 0.097$ to $r = 0.378$. The correlation between the two grades were $r = 0.469$.

Table 1. Correlations between Observed Variables.

	NS_1	NS_2	AN_1	AN_2	UN_1	UN_2	Math	Eng
NS_1	4.456							
NS_2	0.787	4.487						
AN_1	0.348	0.297	4.496					
AN_2	0.376	0.347	0.687	4.045				
UN_1	0.383	0.378	0.295	0.366	5.168			
UN_2	0.282	0.319	0.224	0.239	0.688	5.539		
Math	0.349	0.350	0.289	0.378	0.302	0.275		
Eng	0.225	0.205	0.263	0.241	0.135	0.097	0.469	
Means	4.438	3.817	4.196	4.018	4.900	4.411		
Proportions of the grades							1: 0.123 2: 0.311 3: 0.297 4: 0.174 5: 0.096	1: 0.059 2: 0.393 3: 0.338 4: 0.174 5: 0.037

Note. Variances of the continuous variables are given in the diagonal. NS_i = number series, AN_i = verbal analogies, UN_i = unfolding, i = test half, Math = mathematics grade, Eng = English grade.

2.3. Application of the Bifactor Model

In a first step, we analyzed a bifactor model with equal loadings (loadings of 1) on the general and specific factors. All factors were allowed to correlate with the two criterion variables (see Figure 1b). The estimation of this model did not converge—although a bifactor model with equal loadings but without the two criterion variables fitted the data very well ($\chi^2 = 10.121$, $df = 11$, $p = 0.520$). These estimation problems are due to the fact that a bifactor model with equal loadings and covariates is not identified (i.e., it is not possible to get a unique solution for the parameter estimates). Their nonidentifiability can be explained as follows: In a bifactor model with equal loadings, the covariance of an observed indicator of intelligence and a criterion variable is additively decomposed into (a) the covariance of the criterion variable with the g factor and (b) the variance of the criterion variable with a specific factor. Next, a formal proof is presented.

In the model with equal factor loadings, an observed variable Y_{ik} is decomposed in the following way (the first index i refers to the indicator, the second indicator k to the facet):

$$Y_{ik} = G + S_k + E_{ik}$$

Assuming that the error variables E_{ik} are uncorrelated with the criterion variables, the covariance of the observed variables Y_{ik} and a criterion variable C can be decomposed in the following way:

$$Cov(Y_{ik}, C) = Cov(G + S_k + E_{ik},\ C) = Cov(G, C) + Cov(S_k, C)$$

The covariance $Cov(Y_{ik}, C)$ can be easily estimated by the sample covariance. However, because each covariance $Cov(Y_{ik}, C)$ is additively decomposed in essentially the same two components, there is no unique solution to estimate $Cov(G, C)$ independently from $Cov(S_k, C)$. Hence, the model is not identified.

The decomposition of the covariance $Cov(Y_{ik}, C)$ holds for all indicators of intelligence and all specific factors. According to this decomposition there is an infinite number of combinations of $Cov(G, C)$ and $Cov(S_k, C)$. While this formal proof is herein only presented for the covariance of $Cov(Y_{ik}, C)$, it also applies to polyserial correlations considered in the empirical application. In case of polyserial correlations, the variable C refers to the continuous variable that is underlying the observed categorical variable.

The nonidentification of the bifactor model with equal loadings has an important implication for the general research question of whether g factor versus specific factors predict criterion variables. That is, the model can only be identified and the estimation problems only be solved if one fixes one of the covariances to 0, i.e., either $Cov(G, C) = 0$ or $Cov(S_k, C) = 0$. When we fixed $Cov(S_k, C) = 0$ for all three specific factors of our model, the model was identified and fitted the data very well ($\chi^2 = 17.862$, $df = 21$, $p = 0.658$). In this model, the g factor was significantly correlated with the mathematics grades ($r = 0.574$) and the English grades ($r = 0.344$). Consequently, one would conclude that only g is necessary for predicting grades. However, when we fixed $Cov(G, C) = 0$, the respective model was also identified and fitted the data very well ($\chi^2 = 14.373$, $df = 17$, $p = 0.641$). In this model, the g factor was not correlated with the grades; instead all the specific factors were significantly correlated with the mathematics and the English grades (mathematics—NS: $r = 0.519$, AN: $r = 0.572$, UN: $r = 0.452$; English—NS: $r = 0.319$, AN: $r = 0.434$, UN: $r = 0.184$). Hence, this analysis led to exactly the opposite conclusion: The g factor is irrelevant for predicting grades, only specific factors are relevant. It is important to note that both conclusions are arbitrary, and that the model with equal loadings is in no way suitable for analyzing this research question.

The identification of models with freely estimated loadings on the general and specific factors is more complex and depends on the number of indicators and specific factors. If loadings on the g factor are not fixed to be equal, the model with correlating criterion variables (see Figure 1b) is identified (see Appendix A for a more formal discussion of this issue). However, because there are only two indicators for each specific factor, their loadings have to be fixed to 1. The corresponding model fitted the data very well ($\chi^2 = 8.318$, $df = 10$, $p = 0.598$). The estimated parameters of this model are presented in Table 2[1]. All estimated g factor loadings were very high. The correlations of the mathematics grades with the g factor and with the specific factors were similar, but not significantly different from 0. For the English grades, the correlations differed more: The specific factor of verbal analogies showed the highest correlation with the English grades. However, the correlations were also not significantly different from 0. The results showed that neither the g factor nor the specific factors were correlated with the grades. According to these results, cognitive ability would not be a predictor of grades—which would be in contrast to ample research (e.g., [41]). However, it is important to note that the standard errors for the covariances between the factors and the grades were very high, meaning that they were imprecisely estimated. After fixing the correlations between the specific factors and the grades to 0, the model fitted the data very well ($\chi^2 = 16.998$, $df = 16$, $p = 0.386$). In this model, the standard errors for the estimated covariances between the g factor and the grades were much smaller (mathematics: 0.128, English: 0.18). As a result, the g factor was significantly correlated with both grades (mathematics: $r = 0.568$, English: $r = 0.341$). So, in this analysis, g showed strong correlations with the grades whereas the specific factors were irrelevant. However, fixing the correlations of g with the grades to 0 and letting the specific factors correlate with the grades, resulted in the very opposite conclusion. Again, this model showed a very good fit ($\chi^2 = 8.185$, $df = 12$, $p = 0.771$) and the standard errors of the covariances between the specific factors and the grades were lower (between 0.126 and 0.136). This time, however, all specific factors were significantly correlated with all grades (Mathematics—*NS*: $r = 0.570$, *AN*: $r = 0.522$, *UN*: $r = 0.450$; English—*NS*: $r = 0.350$, *AN*: $r = 0.396$, *UN*: $r = 0.183$). While all specific factors were relevant, in this case the g factor was irrelevant for predicting individual differences in school grades.

Table 2. Bifactor Model and Grades.

	G-Factor Loadings	S-Factor Loadings	Residual Variances	Rel		G	NS-S	AN-S	UN-S	Math	Eng
								Covariances			
NS₁	1 **0.651**	1 **0.615**	0.882 (0.176) **0.198**	0.802	G	1.887 (0.481)	0	0	0	*0.286*	*0.150*
NS₂	0.971 (0.098) **0.630**	1 **0.613**	1.022 (0.199) **0.228**	0.772	NS-S	0	1.687 (0.331)	0	0	*0.272*	*0.194*
AN₁	0.759 (0.161) **0.492**	1 **0.620**	1.681 (0.255) **0.374**	0.626	AN-S	0	0	1.726 (0.316)	0	*0.283*	*0.270*
AN₂	0.838 (0.162) **0.573**	1 **0.653**	0.993 (0.217) **0.245**	0.755	UN-S	0	0	0	2.207 (0.441)	*0.212*	*0.058*
UN₁	1.000 (0.199) **0.604**	1 **0.653**	1.074 (0.215) **0.208**	0.792	Math	*0.393* *(0.456)*	*0.353* *(0.445)*	*0.371* *(0.353)*	*0.315* *(0.428)*		
UN₂	0.781 (0.198) **0.456**	1 **0.631**	2.181 (0.334) **0.394**	0.606	Eng	*0.206* *(0.470)*	*0.252* *(0.475)*	*0.355* *(0.384)*	*0.086* *(0.460)*	0.469 (0.055)	

Notes. Parameter estimates, standard errors of unstandardized parameter estimates (in parentheses), standardized parameter estimates (bold type). Covariances (right side of the table) are presented below the diagonal, variances in the diagonal, and correlations above the diagonal. Rel = reliability estimates, NS_i = number series, AN_i = verbal analogies, UN_i = unfolding, i = test half, Math = mathematics grade, Eng = English grade. All parameter estimates are significantly different from 0 ($p < 0.05$) with the exceptions of parameters that are set in italics.

---

[1]   For reasons of parsimony, we present standard errors and significance tests only for unstandardized solutions (across all analyses included in this paper). The corresponding information for the standardized solutions leads to the same conclusions.

We observed the same problem in a multiple regression analysis in which the grades were regressed on the general and specific factors (see Figure 1c). In this model—which yielded the same fit as the model with all correlations—all regression coefficients showed high standard errors and were not significantly different from 0 (see Table 3). Fixing the regression coefficients on all specific factors to 0 led to a fitting model with significant regression coefficients for the *g* factor, whereas fixing the regression coefficients on the *g* factor to 0 resulted in a fitting model with significant regression weights for the specific factors (with exception of the unfolding factor for the English grades). It is important to note that in the multiple regression analysis the *g* factor and the specific factors were uncorrelated. Therefore, the high standard errors in this model cannot be due to multicollinearity. Instead, it shows that there are more fundamental application problems of the bifactor model for predicting criterion variables.

Table 3. Multivariate Regression Analyses with the Mathematics and English Grades as Dependent Variables and the *g* Factor and the Three Specific Factors as Independent Variables.

	Mathematics ($R^2 = 0.284$)		English ($R^2 = 0.113$)	
	b	b_s	*B*	b_s
G	0.205 (0.234)	0.282	0.115 (0.246)	0.158
NS-S	0.213 (0.264)	0.276	0.143 (0.283)	0.186
AN-S	0.218 (0.207)	0.286	0.200 (0.223)	0.264
UN-S	0.145 (0.198)	0.216	0.035 (0.208)	0.051

Notes. Regression parameter estimates (*b*), standard errors of unstandardized regression parameter estimates (in parentheses), standardized regression estimates (b_s), and coefficient of determination (R^2). G = general factor, NS-S = number series specific factor, AN-S = verbal analogies specific factor, UN-S = unfolding specific factor, Math = Mathematics grade, Eng = English grade. None of the estimated parameters are significantly different from 0 (all $p > 0.05$).

3. Alternatives to Extended Bifactor Models

Because the application of bifactor models for predicting criterion variables by facets of intelligence might lead to invalid conclusions, alternative models might be more appropriate for predicting criterion variables by facets of intelligence. We will discuss two alternative approaches. First, we will illustrate the application of an extended first-order factor model and then of an extended bifactor(S-1) model.

3.1. Application of the Extended First-Order Factor Model

In the first-order factor model there is a common factor for all indicators belonging to the same facet of a construct (see Figure 2a). The factors are correlated; the correlations show how distinct or comparable the different facets are. It is a very general model as the correlations of the latent factors are not restricted in any way (e.g., by a common general factor) and it allows us to test whether the facets can be clearly separated in the intended way (e.g., without cross-loadings). An extension of this model to criterion variables is shown in Figure 2b. We applied this model to estimate the correlations between the intelligence facet factors and the grades. Because the two indicators were created through an odd-even split, we assumed that the loadings of the indicators on the factors did not differ between the two indicators. For identification reasons, the default Mplus settings were applied, meaning that the unstandardized factor loadings were fixed to 1 and the mean values of the factors were fixed to 0.

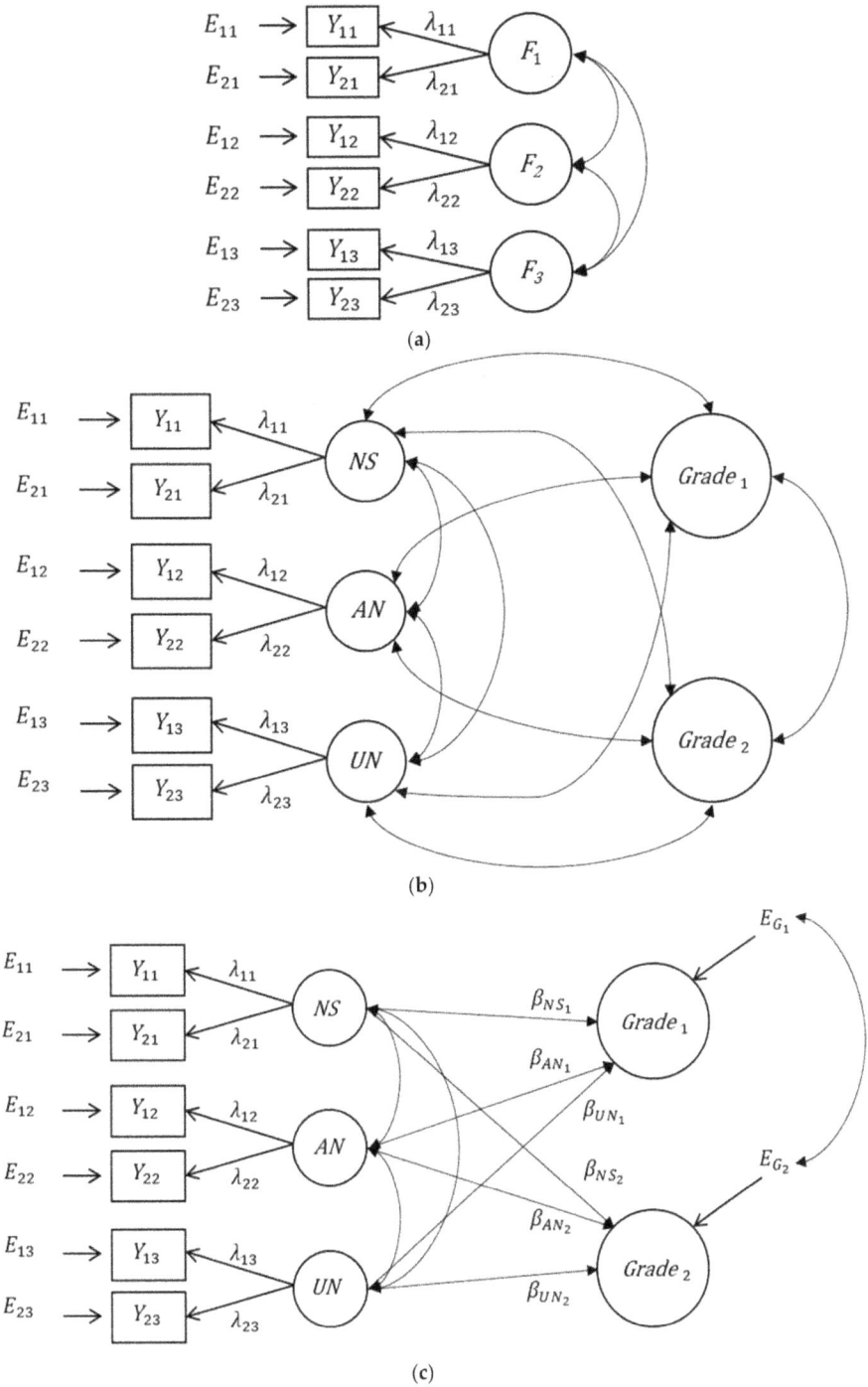

(a)

(b)

(c)

Figure 2. *Cont.*

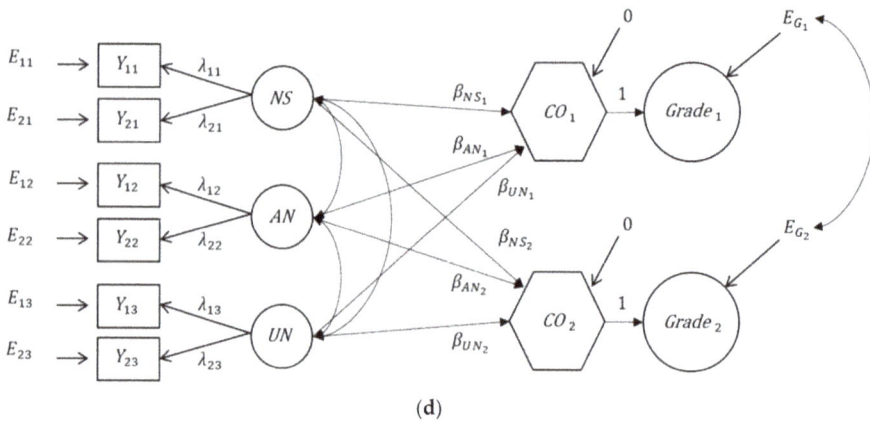

(d)

Figure 2. Modell with correlated first-order factors. (**a**) Model without criterion variables, (**b**) model with correlating criterion variables, (**c**) multiple latent regression model, and (**d**) multiple latent regression model with composite factors. F_k: facet factors, E_{ik}: measurement error variables, *NS*: facet factor number series, *AN*: facet factor verbal analogies, *UN*: facet factor unfolding, CO_1/CO_2: composite factors, E_{G1}/E_{G2}: residuals λ: loading parameters, β: regression coefficients, *i*: indicator, *k*: facet.

This model fitted the data very well ($\chi^2 = 13.929$, $df = 15$, $p = 0.531$) and did not fit significantly worse than a model with unrestricted loadings ($\chi^2 = 9.308$, $df = 12$, $p = 0.676$; scaled χ^2-difference = 2.933, $df = 3$, $p = 0.402$). The results of this analysis are presented in Table 4. The standardized factor loadings and therefore also the reliabilities of the observed indicators were sufficiently high for all observed variables. The correlations between the three facet factors were relatively similar and ranged from $r = 0.408$ to $r = 0.464$. Hence, the facets were sufficiently distinct to consider them as different facets of intelligence. The correlations of the factors with the mathematics grades were all significantly different from 0 and ranged from $r = 0.349$ (unfolding) to $r = 0.400$ (verbal analogies) showing that they differed only slightly between the intelligence facets. The correlations with the English grades were also significantly different from 0, but they differed more strongly between the facets. The strongest correlation of $r = 0.304$ was found for verbal analogies, the correlations with the facets number series and unfolding were $r = 0.242$ and $r = 0.142$, respectively.

The model can be easily extended to predict criterion variables. Figure 2c depicts a multiple regression model with two criterion variables (the two grades in the study presented). The regression coefficients in this model have the same meaning as in a multiple regression analysis. They indicate to which degree a facet of a multidimensional construct contributes to predicting the criterion variable beyond all other facets included in the model. If the regression coefficient of a facet factor is not significantly different from 0, this indicates that this facet is not an important addition to the other facets in predicting the criterion variable. The residuals of the two criterion variables can be correlated. This partial correlation indicates that part of the correlation of the criterion variables that is not due to the common predictor variables. Table 5 shows that the regression coefficients differ between the two grades. Verbal analogies were the strongest predictor of both grades; it predicted both grades almost identically well. The two other intelligence facets had also significant regression weights for the mathematics grades, but their regression weights were small and not significantly different from 0 for the English grades. Consequently, the explained variance also differed between the two grades. Whereas 23.3 percent of the variance of the mathematics grades was explained by the three intelligence facets together, only 10.6 percent of the variance of the English grades was predictable by the three intelligence facets. The residual correlation of $r = 0.390$ indicated that the association of the two grades cannot be perfectly predicted by the three facets of intelligence.

Table 4. Estimates of the Model with Correlated First-order Factors and Grades.

	Factor Loadings	Residual Variances	Rel		Covariances				
					NS	AN	UN	Math	Eng
NS_1	1 **0.889**	0.938 (0.200) **0.211**	0.789	NS	3.519 (0.425)	0.464	0.461	0.394	0.242
NS_2	1 **0.886**	0.967 (0.197) **0.215**	0.785	AN	1.490 (0.274)	2.927 (0.394)	0.408	0.400	0.304
AN_1	1 **0.807**	1.569 (0.290) **0.349**	0.651	UN	1.661 (0.302)	1.338 (0.277)	3.680 (0.493)	0.349	0.142
AN_2	1 **0.851**	1.118 (0.257) **0.276**	0.724	Math	0.740 (0.127)	0.685 (0.126)	0.669 (0.134)		0.469
UN_1	1 **0.844**	1.487 (0.365) **0.288**	0.712	Eng	0.455 (0.136)	0.520 (0.128)	0.272 (0.133)	0.469	
UN_2	1 **0.815**	1.859 (0.390) **0.336**	0.664						

Notes. Parameter estimates, standard errors of unstandardized parameter estimates (in parentheses), and standardized parameter estimates (bold type). Covariances (right side of the table) are presented below the diagonal, variances in the diagonal, and correlations above the diagonal. Rel = reliability estimates, NS_i = number series, AN_i = verbal analogies, UN_i = unfolding, i = test half, Math = mathematics grade, Eng = English grade. All parameter estimates are significantly different from 0 ($p < 0.05$).

Table 5. Multivariate Regression Analyses with Mathematics and English Grades as Dependent Variables and the Three Intelligence Factors as Independent Variables.

	Mathematics ($R^2 = 0.233$)		English ($R^2 = 0.106$)	
	b	b_s	b	b_s
NS	0.113 ** (0.039)	0.213	0.073 (0.046)	0.137
AN	0.140 ** (0.046)	0.239	0.146 ** (0.050)	0.250
UN	0.080 * (0.037)	0.153	−0.012 (0.041)	−0.023

Notes. Regression parameter estimates (b), standard errors of unstandardized regression parameter estimates (in parentheses), standardized regression estimates (b_s), and coefficient of determination (R^2). NS = number series, AN = verbal analogies, UN = unfolding, Math = Mathematics grade, Eng = English grade. ** $p < 0.01$, * $p < 0.05$.

Notably, the multiple regression model can be formulated in a slightly different but equivalent way: A latent composite variable can be introduced reflecting the linear combination of the facet factors for predicting a criterion variable [42]; this model is shown in Figure 2d. In this figure, we use a hexagon to represent a composite variable, an exact linear function of the three composite indicators [43]. The values of this composite variable are the values of the criterion variable predicted by the facet factors. They correspond to the predicted values $\hat{y}$ of a dependent variably Y in a multiple regression analysis. A composite variable combines the information in the single intelligence facets in such a way that all aspects that are relevant for predicting the criterion variable are represented by this composite factor. Consequently, the single facet factors do not contribute to predicting the criterion variable beyond this composite factor. Their contribution is represented by their regression weight determining the composite factor. While this composite factor is not generally necessary for predicting the criterion variables, it might be particularly important in some specific cases. In personnel assessment, for example, one wants to select those individuals whose intelligence scores might best fit the requirements of a vacant position. The composite score may be built to best reflect these specific requirements (if appropriate criterion-related validity studies are available). The composite score thus represents an intelligence score of this person, specifically tailored to the assessment purpose. We argue that—if appropriate evidence allows for it—composite scores that are tailored to the purpose at hand can be more appropriate than aggregating intelligence facets according to their loadings on broader factors (e.g., on the first principal component of all observed intelligence measures or on a *g* factor in a bifactor model). In fact, understanding a broader measure of intelligence as the best combination of intelligence facets is in line with modern approaches of validity [44–47]. According to these approaches, validity is not a property of a psychological test. Rather, a psychometric test can be applied for different purposes (here: predicting different grades) and the information has to be combined and interpreted in the most appropriate way to arrive at valid conclusions. Therefore, it might not always be reasonable to rely on *g* as an underlying variable ("property of a test") such as in a bifactor model, but to look for the best combination of test scores for a specific purpose. Thus, also from a validity-related point-of-view, the bifactor model might be—independently from the estimation problems we have described—a less optimal model.

3.2. Application of the Bifactor(S-1) Model

A bifactor(S-1) model is a variant of a bifactor model in which one specific factor is omitted (see Figure 3a). In this model the *g* factor represents individual differences on the facet that is theoretically selected as the reference facet. Therefore, it is not a general factor as it is assumed in a traditional *g* factor model. Rather, it is intelligence as captured by the reference facet. A specific factor represents that part of a facet that cannot be predicted by the reference facet. Unlike the classical bifactor model, the specific factors in the bifactor(S-1) model can be correlated. This partial correlation indicates whether two facets have something in common that is not shared with the reference facet. A bifactor(S-1) can be defined in such a way that it is a reformulation of the model with correlated first-order factors (see Figure 2a) and shows the same fit [48]. Because first-order factor models usually do not show anomalous results, the bifactor(S-1) model is usually also not affected by the estimation problems found in many applications of the bifactor model [35]. Applying a bifactor(S-1) model may also be a better alternative to bifactor models when it comes to predicting real-world criteria (see Figure 3b,c), because this model avoids the identification and estimation problems inherent in the extended bifactor model.

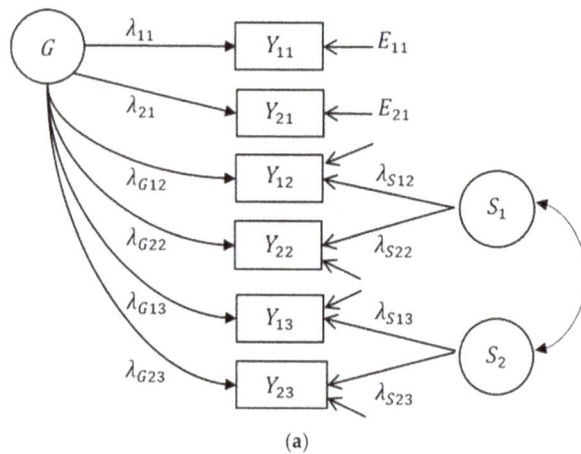

(a)

Figure 3. *Cont.*

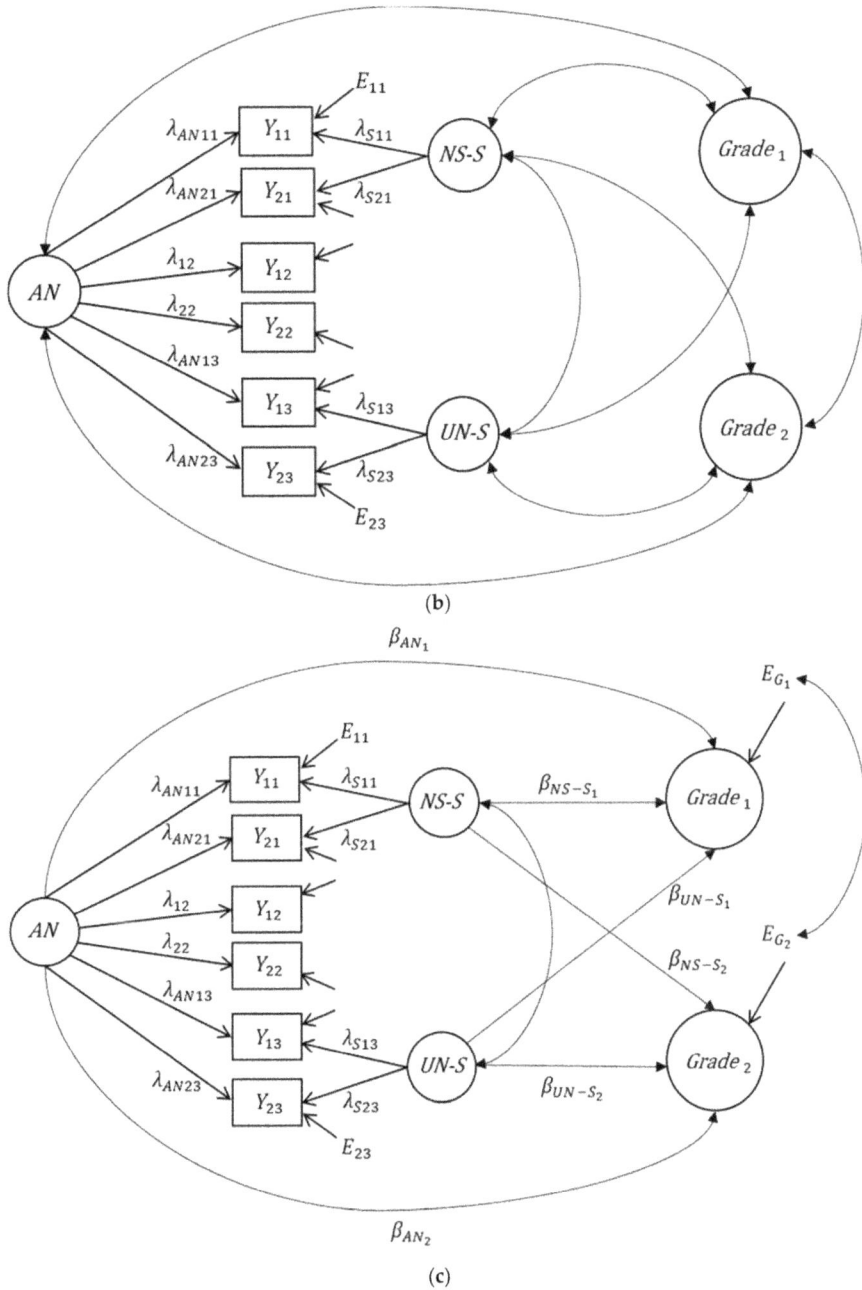

Figure 3. Bifactor(S-1) model and its extensions to criterion variables. (**a**) Bifactor(S-1) model without criterion variables, (**b**) bifactor(S-1) model with correlating criterion variables (grades), and (**c**) multiple latent regression bifactor(S-1) model. The factors of the extended models depicted refer to the empirical application. G: general factor, S_k: specific factors; NS-S: specific factor number series, AN-S: specific factor verbal analogies, UN-S: specific factor unfolding. E_{ik}: measurement error variables, E_{G1}/E_{G2}: residuals, λ: loading parameters, β: regression coefficients, i: indicator, k: facet.

Several researchers have applied the bifactor(S-1) model for predicting criterion variables by cognitive abilities. This was the case even in one of the very early applications of bifactor models of intelligence to predict achievement in different school subjects [49]. In their application of a bifactor(S-1) model, Holzinger and Swineford [49] defined the *g* factor by three reference tests (without indicating a specific factor) and a specific factor by eight tests having loadings on the *g* factor as well as on a specific spatial ability factor.[2] Also Gustafsson and Balke [2] selected one indicator (letter grouping) to define the *g* factor of aptitudes. Other examples of applying bifactor(S-1) models are Brunner's [17] and Saß et al.'s [21] studies, in which a *g* factor of cognitive abilities was defined by fluid ability. Likewise, Benson et al. [15] defined their *g* factor of cognitive abilities by the test story completion. Notably, many applications of the standard bifactor model are essentially bifactor(S-1) models, because often one of the specific factors in the standard bifactor model does not have substantive variance (see [35]). In such cases, the specific factor without substantive variance becomes the reference facet and defines the meaning of the *g* factor. Unfortunately, this is very rarely stated explicitly in such cases. In bifactor(S-1) models, on the contrary, the *g* factor is theoretically and explicitly defined by a reference facet, i.e., the meaning of *g* depends on the choice of the reference facet. Thus, another advantage of the bifactor(S-1) model is that the researcher explicitly determines the meaning of the reference facet factor and communicates it. Moreover, it avoids estimation problems that are related to overfactorization (i.e., specifying a factor that has no variance).

In the bifactor(S-1) model, the regression coefficients for predicting criterion variables by facets of intelligence have a special meaning. We will discuss their meaning by referring to the empirical example presented. For applying the bifactor(S-1) model, one facet has to be chosen as the reference facet. In the current analyses, we chose the facet verbal analogies as the reference facet, because it was most strongly correlated with both grades. However, the reference facet can also be selected on a theoretical basis. The bifactor(S-1) model then tested whether the remaining facets contribute to the prediction of grades above and beyond the reference facet. Because the first-order model showed that the indicators did not differ in their factor loadings, we also assumed that the indicators of a facet showed equal factor loadings in the bifactor(S-1) model.

The fit of the bifactor(S-1) model with the two grades as correlated criterion variables (see Figure 2a) was equivalent to the first-order factor model ($\chi^2 = 13.929$, $df = 15$, $p = 0.531$). This result reflects that both models are simply reformulations of each other. In addition, the correlations between the reference facet and the two grades did not differ from the correlations that were observed in the first-order model. This shows that the meaning of the reference facet does not change from one model to the other. There is, however, an important difference between both models. In the bifactor(S-1) model, the non-reference factors are residualized with respect to the reference facet. Consequently, the meaning of the non-reference facets and their correlations with the criterion variables change. Specifically, the correlations between the specific factors of the bifactor(S-1) model and the grades indicate whether the non-reference factors contain variance that is not shared with the reference facet, but that is shared with the grades. The correlations between the specific factors of the bifactor(S-1) model and the grades are part (semi-partial) correlations (i.e., correlations between the grades, on the one hand side, and the non-reference facets that are residualized with respect to the reference facet, on the other hand side).

The estimated parameters of the bifactor(S-1) model when applied to the empirical example are presented in Table 6. All observed intelligence variables showed substantive loadings on the common factor (i.e., verbal analogies reference facet factor). The standardized loadings of the observed

---

[2]   From a historical point of view this early paper is also interesting for the debate on the role of general and specific factors. It showed that achievements in school subjects that do not belong to the science or language spectrum such as shops and crafts as well as drawing were more strongly correlated with the specific spatial ability factor ($r = 0.461$ and $r = 0.692$) than with the general factor ($r = 0.219$ and $r = 0.412$), whereas the *g* factor was more strongly correlated with all other school domains (between $r = 0.374$ and $r = 0.586$) than the specific factor (between $r = -0.057$ and $r = 0.257$).

verbal analogies indicators were identical to those obtained from the first-order factor model (because the reference facet factor is identical to the first-order factor verbal analogies). The standardized factor loadings of the non-reference factor indicators were smaller (between 0.332 and 0.412); they can be interpreted as correlations between the indicators of the other non-reference facets (i.e., number series and unfolding) and the common verbal analogies factor (i.e., reference facet). The standardized loadings pertaining to the specific factors were higher (between 0.744 and 0.787) showing that the non-reference facets indicators assessed a specific part of these facets that was not shared with the common verbal reasoning factor. The common verbal reasoning factor was strongly correlated with the mathematics grades ($r = 0.400$) and the English grades ($r = 0.304$). Significant correlations were obtained between the specific factors and the mathematics grades ($r = 0.203$ and $r = 0.235$), but not between the specific factors and the English grades. Hence, number series and unfolding were not important for understanding individual differences in English grades, if individual differences in verbal analogies were controlled for.

Table 6. Bifactor(*S*-1) Model with Correlated First-order Factors and Grades.

	G-Factor Loadings	S-Factor Loadings	Residual Variances	Rel		NS-S	AN	UN-S	Math	Eng
NS_1	0.509 (0.083) **0.412**	1 **0.787**	0.938 (0.200) **0.211**	0.789	NS-S	2.760 (0.333)	0	0.337	0.235	*0.114*
NS_2	0.509 (0.083) **0.411**	1 **0.784**	0.968 (0.197) **0.216**	0.784	AN	0	2.928 (0.394)	0	0.400	0.304
AN_1	1 **0.807**		1.568 (0.290) **0.349**	0.651	UN-S	0.980 (0.244)	0	3.069 (0.442)	0.203	*0.020*
AN_2	1 **0.851**		1.117 (0.257) **0.276**	0.724	Math	0.391 (0.110)	0.685 (0.126)	0.356 (0.124)		
UN_1	0.457 (0.084) **0.344**	1 **0.771**	1.487 (0.365) **0.288**	0.712	Eng	*0.190* (0.121)	0.520 (0.128)	*0.035* (0.123)	0.469 (0.055)	
UN_2	0.781 (0.084) **0.332**	1 **0.744**	1.858 (0.390) **0.336**	0.664						

Notes. Parameter estimates, standard errors of unstandardized parameter estimates (in parentheses), and standardized parameter estimates (bold type). Covariances (right side of the table) are presented below the diagonal, variances in the diagonal, and correlations above the diagonal. Rel = reliability estimates, NS_i = umber series, AN_i = verbal analogies, UN_i = unfolding, i = test half, AN = verbal analogies reference facet factor, NS-S = number series specific factor, UN-S = unfolding specific factor, Math = Mathematics grade, Eng = English grade. All parameter estimates are significantly different from 0 ($p < 0.05$) with the exceptions of parameters that are set in italics.

An extension of the bifactor(*S*-1) model to a multiple regression model is depicted in Figure 3c. The estimated parameters are presented in Table 7. For mathematics grades, the results show that the specific factors have a predictive power above and beyond the common verbal analogies reference factor. This was not the case for English grades. The differences between the bifactor(*S*-1) regression model and the first-order factor regression model can be illustrated by comparing the unstandardized regression coefficients in Tables 3 and 7. They only differ for verbal analogies, the facet taken as reference in the bifactor(*S*-1) model. Whereas in the first-order factor model, the regression coefficient of the verbal analogies facet indicates its predictive power above and beyond the two other facets, its regression coefficient in the bifactor(*S*-1) model equals the regression coefficient in a simple regression model (because it is not corrected for its correlation with the remaining non-reference facets). Therefore, in the first-order factor model, the regression coefficient of verbal analogies depends on the other facets considered. If other facets were added to the model, this would affect the regression coefficient of verbal analogies (assuming that the added facets are correlated with verbal analogies). Hence, in order to compare the influence of verbal analogies on the grades across different studies, it is always necessary to take all other included facets into consideration. In the bifactor(S-1) model, however, the regression coefficient of verbal analogies, the reference facet, does not depend on other facets. Adding other facets of intelligence would not change the regression coefficient of verbal analogies. As a result, the regression coefficient of verbal analogies for predicting the same criterion variables can be compared across different studies without considering all other facets.

Table 7. Multivariate Regression analyses with the Mathematics and English Grades as Dependent Variables and the Three Factors of the Bifactor(S-1) Model as Independent Variables (Reference Facet = Verbal Analogies).

	Mathematics ($R^2 = 0.233$)		English ($R^2 = 0.106$)	
	b	b_s	b	b_s
AN	0.234 ** (0.038)	0.400	0.178 ** (0.040)	0.304
NS-S	0.113 ** (0.046)	0.188	0.073 (0.046)	0.122
UN-S	0.080 * (0.037)	0.140	−0.012 (0.041)	−0.021

Note. Regression parameter estimates (b), standard errors of unstandardized regression parameter estimates (in parentheses), standardized regression estimates (b_s), and coefficient of determination (R^2). AN = verbal analogies reference facet factor, NS-S = number series specific factor, UN-S = unfolding specific factor, Math = Mathematics grade, Eng = English grade. ** $p < 0.01$, * $p < 0.05$.

It is important to note that the correlations and the regression coefficients in the bifactor(S-1) model can change if one selects another facet as the reference facet. When we changed the reference facet in our empirical example, however, neither the fit of the bifactor(S-1) model nor did the explained variance in the criterion variables changed. When we used number series as reference facet, for example, the regression coefficient of verbal analogies—now considered a specific facet—significantly predicted English grades, in addition to the reference facet (see Table 8). When predicting mathematics grades, the specific factors of verbal analogies and unfolding had an additional effect. Note that the choice of the reference facet depends on the research question and can also differ between criterion variables (e.g., verbal analogies might be chosen as reference facet for language grades and number series as reference facet for mathematics and science grades).

Table 8. Multivariate Regression analyses with the Mathematics and English Grades as Dependent Variables and the Three Factors of the Bifactor(S-1) Model as Independent Variables (Reference Facet = Number Series).

	Mathematics ($R^2 = 0.233$)		English ($R^2 = 0.106$)	
	b	b_s	b	b_s
NS	0.210 ** (0.031)	0.394	0.129 ** (0.037)	0.242
AN-S	0.140 ** (0.046)	0.212	0.146 ** (0.050)	0.221
UN-S	0.080 * (0.037)	0.136	−0.012 (0.041)	−0.021

Note. Regression parameter estimates (b), standard errors of unstandardized regression parameter estimates (in parentheses), standardized regression estimates (b_s), and coefficient of determination (R^2). NS = number series reference facet factor, AS-S = verbal analogies specific factor, UN-S = unfolding specific factor, Math = Mathematics grade, Eng = English grade. ** $p < 0.01$, * $p < 0.05$.

4. Discussion

The bifactor model has become a standard model for analyzing general and specific factors [35,37]. One major advantage of the bifactor model is that all factors are uncorrelated. If one extends the model to a multiple regression framework and uses this model to predict criterion variables by general and specific factors, then the general and specific factors are independent sources of prediction. So, the problem of multicollinearity is avoided. Hence, the regression weights indicate to which degree general and specific abilities are important for predicting criterion variables. However, our empirical application revealed severe identification and estimation problems which strongly limit the applicability of the bifactor model for predicting criterion variables. First, the bifactor model with criterion variables as covariates is not identified if (a) the indicators do not differ in their loadings on the general and specific factors, and (b) both the general and specific factors are correlated with the criterion variables. In the herein conducted empirical application of the bifactor model, the indicators did not differ significantly in their loadings. Therefore, the extended bifactor model with equal loadings could not be applied. Equal loadings might be rather common in intelligence research, because many authors of intelligence tests might base their item selection on the Rasch model [50], also called the one-parameter logistic model. The Rasch model has many advantages such as specific objectivity, the fact that item parameters can be independently estimated from person parameters and that the total score is a sufficient statistic for the ability parameter. Particularly, applications of bifactor models on item parcels or items that do not differ in their discrimination—as is the case in the one-parameter logistic model—will result in identification problems. The same is true for tests developed on the basis of the classical test theory, where equal factor loadings are desirable for test authors (mostly because of the ubiquitous use of Cronbach's alpha, which is only a measure of test score reliability if the items do not differ in their loadings). Hence, applying well-constructed tests in research on intelligence might often result in a situation where the loadings are equal or similar.

However, in the case of equal loadings, the extended bifactor model is only identified if the correlations (or regression weights) of either the general factor with the criterion variables or of the specific factors with the criterion variables are fixed to 0. This has a serious implication for research on general vs. specific factors predicting real-world criteria: The bifactor model is not suitable for deciding whether the general or the specific factors are more important for predicting criterion variables. As we have shown in the empirical application, one can specify the model in such a way that either the *g* factor or the specific factors are the relevant source of individual differences in the criterion variables, thereby making this model arbitrary for determining the relative importance of *g* versus specific abilities. In order to get an identified bifactor model, we had to freely estimate the factor loadings of the general factor. However, even for this (then identified) model, the standard errors of the correlation and regression coefficients were so large that none of the coefficients were significant—although generally strong associations between intelligence facets and school grades existed. Hence, applying the bifactor model with criterion (or other) variables as covariates can result in invalid conclusions about the importance of general and specific factors.

It is important to note that the high standard errors are not due to multicollinearity, but seem to be a property of the model itself, as the estimated factor loadings were close to the situation of non-identification (i.e., almost equal). Fixing either the correlations between the grades and the general factor or between the grades and the specific factors results in lower standard errors and significant correlations and regression weights. Again, however, it cannot be appropriately decided whether the general factor or the specific factors are the relevant source of individual differences. This fact even offers some possibilities for misuse. For example, proponents of the *g* factor might report the fit coefficients of the model with all correlation coefficients estimated and with the correlation coefficients of the specific factors fixed to zero. They might argue (and statistically test) that the two models fit equally well and, therefore, report only the results of the reduced model showing significant *g* factor correlations. This would lead to the conclusion that the specific factors are irrelevant for predicting criterion variables. Conversely, proponents of specific factors might apply the same strategy and use the same arguments to show that *g* is irrelevant (e.g., only measuring response styles) and only the specific factors are relevant. According to our analyses, both conclusions are arbitrary and not valid. Because of this arbitrariness, the question arises what the general factor and the specific factors mean.

Because of the strong limitations of the extended bifactor model, we proposed two alternative approaches. The first alternative is an extension of the first-order factor model to a latent multiple regression model in which the criterion variables are regressed on different facet factors. The regression weights in such a model reflect the impact of a facet on a criterion variable, after controlling for all other facets. This is equivalent to residualizing a facet with respect to all other facets and removing that part of a facet that is already shared with all remaining facets in the model. Thus, a regression weight of 0 means that the facet does not contribute to the prediction of the criterion variable above and beyond all other facets in the model. When applied to general and specific abilities, we have shown that the multiple regression model can be formulated in such a way that a composite factor is defined as the best linear combination of different facets. The importance of a specific facet is represented by the weight with which the specific facet contributes to the composite factor. Because of the properties of the multiple regression models, the meaning of the composite factor can differ between different criterion variables. That means that depending on the purpose of a study, the composite factor always represents the best possible combination of the information (specific abilities) available. Our application showed that we need different composite factors to predict grades in mathematics and English. For English grades, the composite factor was essentially determined by the facet verbal analogies, whereas a linear combination of all three facets predicted mathematics grades. From the perspective of criterion-related validity, it might not always be best to rely on *g* as an underlying variable ("property of a test") but to use the best combination of test scores for a specific purpose, which might be viewed as the best exploitation of the available information.

The first-order factor model can be reformulated to a model with a reflective general factor on which all observed indicators load. In such a bifactor(*S*-1) model, the first-order factor of a facet taken as reference facet defines the common factor. The indicators of the non-reference specific abilities are regressed on the reference factor. The specific part of a non-reference facet that is not determined by the common reference factor is represented by a specific factor. The specific factors can be correlated. If one puts certain restrictions on the parameters in the bifactor(*S*-1) model, as done in the application, the model is data equivalent to the first-order factor model (for a deeper discussion see [48]). The main difference to the first-order factor model is that the regression weight of the reference facet factor (the common factor) does not depend on the other facets (in a regression model predicting criterion variables). The regression weight equals the regression coefficient in a simple regression analysis, because the reference factor is uncorrelated with all other factors. However, the regression coefficients of the remaining facets represent that part of a facet that does not depend on the reference facet. Depending on the reference facets chosen the regression weights of the specific factors might differ. Because the specific factors can be correlated a regression coefficient of a specific factor indicates the contribution of the specific factor beyond the other specific factors (and the reference facet).

The bifactor(*S*-1) model is particularly useful if a meaningful reference facet exists. For example, if an intelligence researcher aims to contrast different facets of intelligence against one reference facet (e.g., fluid intelligence) that she or he considers as basic, the bifactor(*S*-1) model would be the appropriate model. For example, Baumert, Brunner, Lüdtke, and Trautwein [51] analyzed the cognitive abilities assessed in the international PISA study using a nested factor model which equals a bifactor(*S*-1) model. They took the figure and word analogy tests as indicators of a common reference intelligence factor (analogies) with which verbal and mathematical abilities (represented by a specific factor respectively) were contrasted. The common intelligence factor had a clear meaning (analogies) that is a priori defined by the researcher. Therefore, researchers are aware of what they are measuring. This is in contrast to applications of *g* models in which specific factors have zero variance as a result of the analysis. For example, Johnson, Bouchard, Krueger, McGue, and Gottesman [52] could show that the *g* factors derived from three test batteries were very strongly correlated. They defined a *g* factor as a second order factor for each test battery. In the model linking the three test batteries, each *g* factor has a very strong loading (1.00, 0.99, 0.95) with a verbal ability facet. Given these high factor loadings, there is no room for a specific factor for verbal abilities and *g* essentially equals verbal abilities. Therefore, the three very strongly related *g* factors were three verbal ability factors. Johnson, te Nijenhuis, and Bouchard [53] could confirm that the *g* factors of three other test batteries were also strongly correlated. In their analysis, the three *g* factors were most strongly linked to first-order factors assessing mechanical and geometrical abilities. Consequently, the meaning of the *g* factors might differ between the two studies. The meaning of *g* has always been referred to from looking at complex loading structures and often it reduces to one stronger reference facet. An advantage of a priori defining a reference facet has the advantage that the meaning of the common factor is clear and can be easily communicated to the scientific community. The empirical application presented in this paper showed that verbal analogies might be such an outstanding facet for predicting school grades. If one selects this facet as the reference facet, the specific factors of the other facets do not contribute to predicting English grades, but they contribute to mathematics grades.

5. Conclusions and Recommendations

Given the identification and estimation problems, the utility of the bifactor model for predicting criterion variables by general and specific factors is questionable. Further research is needed to scrutinize under which conditions a bifactor model with additional correlating criterion variables can be appropriately applied. At the very least, when the bifactor model is applied to analyze correlations with general and specific factors, it is necessary to report all correlations and regressions weights as well as their standard errors in order to decide whether or not the bifactor model was appropriately applied in a specific research context. In applications in which the correlations of some specific factors with criterion variables are fixed to 0 and are not reported, it remains unclear whether one would not have also found a well-fitting model with substantive correlations for all specific factors and non-significant correlations for the general factor. In the current paper, we recommend applying two alternative models, first-order factor models and bifactor(S-1) models. The choice between first-order factor models and bifactor(S-1) models depends on the availability of a facet that can be taken as reference. If there is a meaningful reference facet or a facet that is of specific scientific interest, the bifactor(S-1) model would be the model of choice. If one does not want to make a distinction between the different specific facets, the first-order factor model can be applied.

Author Contributions: S.K. prepared the data set, M.E. did the statistical analyses. All authors contributed to the text.

Conflicts of Interest: The authors declare no conflict of interest.

Appendix A

In the text, it is shown that a bifactor model with a correlating criterion variable is not identified if the indicators do not differ in their loading parameters. In this appendix, it will be shown that a bifactor model with a correlating criterion variable is identified if the loadings on the general factor differ. We only refer to the covariance structure. In all models of confirmatory factor analysis, either one loading parameter per factor or the variance of the factor has to be fixed to a positive value to get an identified model. We chose the Mplus default setting with fixing one loading parameter per factor to 1. Because there are only two indicators per specific factor and the specific factors are not correlated with the remaining specific factors, we fixed all factor loadings of the specific factors to 1. Whereas the nonidentification of bifactor models with equal loadings refers to all bifactor models independently of the number of indicators and specific facets, the identification of models with freely estimated loadings on the general and specific factors depends on the number of indicators and specific factors. The proof of identification of the bifactor model with correlating criterion variables in general goes beyond the scope of the present research and will not be provided. We only consider the models applied in the empirical application.

In the following, a general factor is denoted with G, the facet-specific factors are denoted with S_k, the observed variables with Y_{ik}, and measurement error variables with E_{ik}. The first index i refers to the indicator, the second indicator k to the facet. Hence, Y_{11} is the first indicator of the first facet considered. A criterion variable is denoted with C. We consider only one criterion variable. We only consider models in which the criterion variables are correlated with the factors. Because the regression coefficients in a multiple regression model are functions of the covariances, the identification issues also apply to the multiple regression model. Moreover, we will only consider the identification of the covariances between the criterion variables and the general as well as specific factors because the identification of the bifactor model itself has been shown elsewhere (e.g., [54]). In the models applied, it is assumed that the criterion variables are categorical variables with underlying continuous variables. The variables C are the underlying continuous variables. If the criterion variable is a continuous variable, C denotes the continuous variable itself. In the model with free loadings on the general factor, the observed variables can be decomposed in the following way:

$$Y_{ik} = \lambda_{ik}G + S_k + E_{ik}$$

with $\lambda_{11} = 1$. The covariance of an observed variable Y_{ik} with the criterion can be decomposed in the following way:

$$Cov(Y_{ik}, C) = Cov(\lambda_{ik}G + S_k + E_{ik},\ C) = \lambda_{ik}Cov(G,C) + Cov(S_k, C)$$

with

$$Cov(Y_{11}, C) = Cov(G + S_1 + E_{11},\ C) = Cov(G,C) + Cov(S_1, C)$$

For the difference between the two covariances $Cov(Y_{11}, C)$ and $Cov(Y_{21}, C)$ the following decomposition holds:

$$Cov(Y_{11}, C) - Cov(Y_{21}, C) = Cov(G,C) + Cov(S_1, C) - \lambda_{21}Cov(G,C) - Cov(S_1, C)$$
$$= Cov(G,C) - \lambda_{21}Cov(G,C) = (1 - \lambda_{21})Cov(G,C)$$

Consequently, the covariance between the general factor and the criterion variable is identified by

$$Cov(G,C) = [Cov(Y_{11}, C) - Cov(Y_{21}, C)]/(1 - \lambda_{21})$$

with

$$\lambda_{21} = Cov(Y_{21}, Y_{12})/Cov(Y_{11}, Y_{12})$$

The covariances between the three specific factors and the criterion variable are identified by the following equations:

$$Cov(S_1, C) = Cov(Y_{21}, C) - \lambda_{21}Cov(G,C) = Cov(Y_{21}, C) - \frac{Cov(Y_{21}, Y_{12})[Cov(Y_{11}, C) - Cov(Y_{21}, C)]}{Cov(Y_{11}, Y_{12})(1 - Cov(Y_{21}, Y_{12})/Cov(Y_{11}, Y_{12}))}$$

$$Cov(S_2, C) = Cov(Y_{12}, C) - \lambda_{12}Cov(G,C) = Cov(Y_{21}, C) - \frac{Cov(Y_{12}, Y_{13})[Cov(Y_{11}, C) - Cov(Y_{21}, C)]}{Cov(Y_{11}, Y_{13})(1 - Cov(Y_{21}, Y_{12})/Cov(Y_{11}, Y_{12}))}$$

$$Cov(S_3, C) = Cov(Y_{13}, C) - \lambda_{13}Cov(G,C) = Cov(Y_{13}, C) - \frac{Cov(Y_{13}, Y_{12})[Cov(Y_{11}, C) - Cov(Y_{21}, C)]}{Cov(Y_{11}, Y_{12})(1 - Cov(Y_{21}, Y_{12})/Cov(Y_{11}, Y_{12}))}$$

References

1. Spearman, C. General Intelligence objectively determined and measured. *Am. J. Psychol.* **1904**, *15*, 201–293. [CrossRef]
2. Gustafsson, J.E.; Balke, G. General and specific abilities as predictors of school achievement. *Multivar. Behav. Res.* **1993**, *28*, 407–434. [CrossRef] [PubMed]

3. Kuncel, N.R.; Hezlett, S.A.; Ones, D.S. Academic performance, career potential, creativity, and job performance: Can one construct predict them all? *J. Pers. Soc. Psychol.* **2004**, *86*, 148–161. [CrossRef] [PubMed]

4. Kell, H.J.; Lang, J.W.B. Specific abilities in the workplace: More important than g? *J. Intell.* **1993**, *5*, 13. [CrossRef]

5. Carretta, T.R.; Ree, M.J. General and specific cognitive and psychomotor abilities in personnel selection: The prediction of training and job performance. *Int. J. Sel. Assess.* **2000**, *8*, 227–236. [CrossRef]

6. Ree, M.J.; Earles, J.A.; Teachout, M.S. Predicting job performance: Not much more than g. *J. Appl. Psychol.* **1994**, *79*, 518–524. [CrossRef]

7. Ree, J.M.; Carretta, T.R. G2K. *Hum. Perform.* **2002**, *15*, 3–23.

8. Murphy, K. What can we learn from "Not much more than g"? *J. Intell.* **2017**, *5*, 8–14. [CrossRef]

9. Lang, J.W.B.; Kersting, M.; Hülsheger, U.R.; Lang, J. General mental ability, narrower cognitive abilities, and job performance: The perspective of the nested-factors model of cognitive abilities. *Pers. Psychol.* **2010**, *63*, 595–640. [CrossRef]

10. Rindermann, H.; Neubauer, A.C. Processing speed, intelligence, creativity, and school performance: Testing of causal hypotheses using structural equation models. *Intelligence* **2004**, *32*, 573–589. [CrossRef]

11. Goertz, W.; Hülsheger, U.R.; Maier, G.W. The validity of specific cognitive abilities for the prediction of training success in Germany: A meta-analysis. *J. Pers. Psychol.* **2014**, *13*, 123. [CrossRef]

12. Ziegler, M.; Dietl, E.; Danay, E.; Vogel, M.; Bühner, M. Predicting training success with general mental ability, specific ability tests, and (un)structured interviews: A meta-analysis with unique samples. *Int. J. Sel. Assess.* **2011**, *19*, 170–182. [CrossRef]

13. Holzinger, K.; Swineford, F. The bi-factor method. *Psychometrika* **1937**, *2*, 41–54. [CrossRef]

14. Beaujean, A.A.; Parkin, J.; Parker, S. Comparing Cattewll-Horn-Carroll factor models: Differences between bifactor and higher order factor models in predicting language achievement. *Psychol. Assess.* **2014**, *26*, 789–805. [CrossRef] [PubMed]

15. Benson, N.F.; Kranzler, J.H.; Floyd, R.G. Examining the integrity of measurement of cognitive abilities in the prediction of achievement: Comparisons and contrasts across variables from higher-order and bifactor models. *J. Sch. Psychol.* **2016**, *58*, 1–19. [CrossRef] [PubMed]

16. Betts, J.; Pickard, M.; Heistad, D. Investigating early literacy and numeracy: Exploring the utility of the bifactor model. *Sch. Psychol. Q.* **2011**, *26*, 97–107. [CrossRef]

17. Brunner, M. No g in education? *Learn. Individ. Differ.* **2008**, *18*, 152–165. [CrossRef]

18. Christensen, A.P.; Silvia, P.J.; Nusbaum, E.C.; Beaty, R.E. Clever people: Intelligence and humor production ability. *Psychol. Aesthet. Creat. Arts* **2018**, *12*, 136–143. [CrossRef]

19. Immekus, J.C.; Atitya, B. The predictive validity of interim assessment scores based on the full-information bifactor model for the prediction of end-of-grade test performance. *Educ. Assess.* **2016**, *21*, 176–195. [CrossRef]

20. McAbee, S.T.; Oswald, F.L.; Connelly, B.S. Bifactor models of personality and college student performance: A broad versus narrow view. *Eur. J. Pers.* **2014**, *28*, 604–619. [CrossRef]

21. Saß, S.; Kampa, N.; Köller, O. The interplay of g and mathematical abilities in large-scale assessments across grades. *Intelligence* **2017**, *63*, 33–44. [CrossRef]

22. Schult, J.; Sparfeldt, J.R. Do non-g factors of cognitive ability tests align with specific academic achievements? A combined bifactor modeling approach. *Intelligence* **2016**, *59*, 96–102. [CrossRef]

23. Silvia, P.J.; Beaty, R.E.; Nusbaum, E.C. Verbal fluency and creativity: General and specific contributions of broad retrieval ability (Gr) factors to divergent thinking. *Intelligence* **2013**, *41*, 328–340. [CrossRef]

24. Silvia, P.J.; Thomas, K.S.; Nusbaum, E.C.; Beaty, R.E.; Hodges, D.A. How does music training predict cognitive abilities? A bifactor approach to musical expertise and intelligence. *Psychol. Aesthet. Creat. Arts* **2016**, *10*, 184–190. [CrossRef]

25. Gunnell, K.E.; Gaudreau, P. Testing a bi-factor model to disentangle general and specific factors of motivation in self-determination theory. *Pers. Individ. Differ.* **2015**, *81*, 35–40. [CrossRef]

26. Stefansson, K.K.; Gestdottir, S.; Geldhof, G.J.; Skulason, S.; Lerner, R.M. A bifactor model of school engagement: Assessing general and specific aspects of behavioral, emotional and cognitive engagement among adolescents. *Int. J. Behav. Dev.* **2016**, *40*, 471–480. [CrossRef]

27. Wang, M.-T.; Fredericks, J.A.; Ye, F.; Hofkens, T.L.; Schall Linn, J. The math and science engagement scales: Scale development, validation, and psychometric properties. *Learn. Instr.* **2016**, *43*, 16–26. [CrossRef]

28. Byllesby, B.M.; Elhai, J.D.; Tamburrino, M.; Fine, T.H.; Cohen, C.; Sampson, L.; Shirley, E.; Chan, P.K.; Liberzon IGalea, S.; Calabrese, J.R. General distress is more important than PTSD's cognition and mood alterations factor in accounting for PTSD and depression's comorbidity. *J. Affect. Disord.* **2017**, *211*, 118–123. [CrossRef] [PubMed]

29. Ogg, J.A.; Bateman, L.; Dedrick, R.F.; Suldo, S.M. The relationship between life satisfaction and ADHD symptoms in middle school students: Using a bifactor model. *J. Atten. Disord.* **2016**, *20*, 390–399. [CrossRef] [PubMed]

30. Subica, A.M.; Allen, J.G.; Frueh, B.C.; Elhai, J.D.; Fowler, C.J. Disentangling depression and anxiety in relation to neuroticism, extraversion, suicide, and self-harm among adult psychiatric inpatients with serious mental illness. *Br. J. Clin. Psychol.* **2015**, *55*, 349–370. [CrossRef] [PubMed]

31. Furtner, M.R.; Rauthmann, J.F.; Sachse, P. Unique self-leadership: A bifactor model approach. *Leadership* **2015**, *11*, 105–125. [CrossRef]

32. Chen, F.F.; Hayes, A.; Carver, C.S.; Laurenceau, J.P.; Zhang, Z. Modeling general and specific variance in multifaceted constructs: A comparison of the bifactor model to other approaches. *J. Pers.* **2012**, *80*, 219–251. [CrossRef] [PubMed]

33. Debusscher, J.; Hofmans, J.; De Fruyt, F. The multiple face(t)s of state conscientiousness: Predicting task performance and organizational citizenship behavior. *J. Res. Pers.* **2017**, *69*, 78–85. [CrossRef]

34. Chiu, W.; Won, D. Relationship between sport website quality and consumption intentions: Application of a bifactor model. *Psychol. Rep.* **2016**, *118*, 90–106. [CrossRef] [PubMed]

35. Eid, M.; Geiser, C.; Koch, T.; Heene, M. Anomalous results in g-factor models: Explanations and alternatives. *Psychol. Methods* **2017**, *22*, 541–562. [CrossRef] [PubMed]

36. Brunner, M.; Nagy, G.; Wilhelm, O. A tutorial on hierarchically structured constructs. *J. Pers.* **2012**, *80*, 796–846. [CrossRef] [PubMed]

37. Reise, S.P. The rediscovery of the bifactor measurement models. *Multivar. Behav. Res.* **2012**, *47*, 667–696. [CrossRef] [PubMed]

38. Kell, H.J.; Lang, J.W.B. The great debate: General abilitiy and specific abilities in the prediction of important outcomes. *J. Intell.* **2018**, *6*, 24.

39. Kersting, M.; Althoff, K.; Jäger, A.O. *WIT-2. Der Wilde-Intelligenztest. Verfahrenshinweise*; Hogrefe: Göttingen, Germany, 2008.

40. Muthén, L.K.; Muthén, B.O. *Mplus User's Guide*, 8th ed.; Muthén & Muthén: Los Angeles, CA, USA, 1998.

41. Roth, B.; Becker, N.; Romeyke, S.; Schäfer, S.; Domnick, F.; Spinath, F.M. Intelligence and school grades: A meta-analysis. *Intelligence* **2015**, *53*, 118–137. [CrossRef]

42. Bollen, K.A.; Bauldry, S. Three Cs in measurement models: Causal indicators, composite indicators, and covariates. *Psychol. Methods* **2011**, *16*, 265–284. [CrossRef] [PubMed]

43. Grace, J.B.; Bollen, K.A. Representing general theoretical concepts in structural equation models: The role of composite variables. *Environ. Ecol. Stat.* **2008**, *15*, 191–213. [CrossRef]

44. Cronbach, L.J. *Essentials of Psychological Testing*, 3rd ed.; Harper & Row: New York, NY, USA, 1970.

45. Kane, M.T. Validating the interpretations and uses of test scores. *J. Educ. Meas.* **2013**, *50*, 1–73. [CrossRef]

46. Messick, S. Validity. In *Educational Measurement*, 3rd ed.; Linn, R.L., Ed.; Macmillan: New York, NY, USA, 1989; pp. 13–103.

47. Newton, P.; Shaw, S. *Validity in Educational and Psychological Assessment*; Sage: Thousand Oaks, CA, USA, 2014.

48. Geiser, C.; Eid, M.; Nussbeck, F.W. On the meaning of the latent variables in the CT-C(M–1) model: A comment on Maydeu-Olivares & Coffman (2006). *Psychol. Methods* **2008**, *13*, 49–57. [PubMed]

49. Holzinger, K.J.; Swineford, F. The relationship of two bi-factors to achievement in geometry and other subjects. *J. Educ. Psychol.* **1946**, *27*, 257–265. [CrossRef]

50. Rasch, G. *Probabilistic Models for Some Intelligence and Attainment Test*; University of Chicago Press: Chicago, IL, USA, 1980.

51. Baumert, J.; Brunner, M.; Lüdtke, O.; Trautwein, U. Was messen internationale Schulleistungsstudien?—Resultate kumulativer Wissenserwerbsprozesse [What are international school achievement studies measuring? Results of cumulative acquisition of knowledge processes]. *Psychol. Rundsch.* **2007**, *58*, 118–145. [CrossRef]

52. Johnson, W.; Bouchard, T.J., Jr.; Krueger, R.F.; McGue, M.; Gottesman, I.I. Just one g: Consistent results from three test batteries. *Intelligence* **2004**, *32*, 95–107. [CrossRef]

53. Johnson, W.; Te Nijenhuis, J.; Bouchard, T.J., Jr. Still just 1 g: Consistent results from five test batteries. *Intelligence* **2008**, *36*, 81–95. [CrossRef]
54. Steyer, R.; Mayer, A.; Geiser, C.; Cole, D.A. A theory of states and traits: Revised. *Annu. Rev. Clin. Psychol.* **2015**, *11*, 71–98. [CrossRef] [PubMed]

Journal of
Intelligence

MDPI

Article

How Specific Abilities Might Throw '*g*' a Curve: An Idea on How to Capitalize on the Predictive Validity of Specific Cognitive Abilities

Matthias Ziegler * and Aaron Peikert

Psychological Institute, Humboldt-Universität zu Berlin, Unter den Linden 6, 10099 Berlin, Germany;
aaron.peikert@hu-berlin.de
* Correspondence: zieglema@hu-berlin.de

Received: 12 March 2018; Accepted: 17 July 2018; Published: 7 September 2018

Abstract: School grades are still used by universities and employers for selection purposes. Thus, identifying determinants of school grades is important. Broadly, two predictor categories can be differentiated from an individual difference perspective: cognitive abilities and personality traits. Over time, evidence accumulated supporting the notion of the *g*-factor as the best single predictor of school grades. Specific abilities were shown to add little incremental validity. The current paper aims at reviving research on which cognitive abilities predict performance. Based on ideas of criterion contamination and deficiency as well as Spearman's ability differentiation hypothesis, two mechanisms are suggested which both would lead to curvilinear relations between specific abilities and grades. While the data set provided for this special issue does not allow testing these mechanisms directly, we tested the idea of curvilinear relations. In particular, polynomial regressions were used. Machine learning was applied to identify the best fitting models in each of the subjects math, German, and English. In particular, we fitted polynomial models with varying degrees and evaluated their accuracy with a leave-one-out validation approach. The results show that tests of specific abilities slightly outperform the *g*-factor when curvilinearity is assumed. Possible theoretical explanations are discussed.

Keywords: *g*-factor; specific abilities; scholastic performance; school grades; machine learning; curvilinear relations; ability differentiation

1. Introduction

Scholastic performance is an important predictor of later academic success [1,2], health [3], and job success [4]. Moreover, many decisions are based on the grades students achieve in school (e.g., college or university admission). It is therefore not surprising that research has focused its attention on grades. One study by French, Homer, Popovici and Robins [4] looking at educational attainment and later success in life specifically targeted high school GPA as a predictor, recognizing it as an important predictor of later job success. It is also just consequential that much research has been devoted to the predictors of scholastic success, mostly using grades as dependent variable e.g., [5–8]. Here, as in many other fields [9–13], general mental ability or the *g*-factor has often been singled out as the best predictor of scholastic performance [14–16] with specific abilities purportedly adding little or no explained variance [17]. However, this focus on the so-called general factor seems to not take full advantage of the structure of intelligence [18,19], which postulates a hierarchical structure with a multitude of specific abilities located at lower levels beneath a *g*-factor. This hierarchical structure also finds support in brain research [20]. However, research focusing on the predictors of scholastic success now often takes *g* for granted and only looks at other constructs to improve predictions [21–24]. The current special issue, as well as this paper, aims at reviving the debate about specific cognitive abilities and their importance for scholastic success. Building on the concepts of criterion deficiency and contamination [25] as well as on the theory of ability differentiation [26,27], we suggest two mechanisms which both would lead to curvilinear relations between specific abilities and grades. The disregard of such nonlinear models in the past might have yielded the wrong impression about the fidelity of specific abilities with regards to school grades. Additionally, we will also test the idea of such curvilinear relations using a machine learning approach.

1.1. Critique on the g-Factor and Its Use as Single Predictor of Performance

Much of the research on the *g*-factor covers areas outside of the scholastic domain, focusing on academic performance, health, job performance, or longevity. Thus, the critique on *g* also originates from a diverse set of researchers. Possibly the most fundamental critique can be found in studies doubting the sheer existence of *g*. Kovacs and Conway [28]. For example, it was postulated that cognitive tests require several processes and that an overlap of such processes might be the cause for finding *g*. This view has been harshly refuted e.g., [29]. Others have stressed that the strong emphasis on *g* has hindered progress on research of intelligence in its breadth [30]. Schneider and Newman [31] reviewed the literature and suggested six reasons why lower order factors of cognitive ability need to be considered despite the often reported importance of *g*. Their first statement is to point out that the empirical fit of hierarchical and multifactor models of intelligence often outperforms the fit of unidimensional models [32–34]. A fly in the ointment is the low construct reliabilities often observed for scores reflecting specific abilities once the *g*-factor is controlled for [35,36]. This can be seen as a first hint that gains from looking at specific abilities cannot be huge. In fact, Schneider and Newman use these small but nevertheless verifiable incremental contributions as their second reason to further investigate specific cognitive abilities. A meta-analysis by Ziegler et al. [37] looking at the predictive validity of specific ability tests with regards to job training also reports such low but significant values when not considering the principle of compatibility or level of symmetry [38,39]. This principle of compatibility also stated by Schneider and Newman means that predictor and criterion need to have a similar level of symmetry or level of abstraction to find optimal correlations. Thus, specific abilities might be better suited to predict specific performance [40]. Ziegler et al. [37] also showed this for the prediction of training success and motoric abilities. Lang et al. [41] reported similar findings with job performance as the criterion. Another reason for focusing on specific abilities stated by Schneider and Newman are the sound theoretical models and empirical studies supporting the notion of a broad spectrum of second order abilities [19]. Another argument is that the effect of adverse impact can be ameliorated by differentially weighing specific cognitive abilities. Finally, Schneider and Newman point towards bifactor models as a possible means to better gauge the effects of specific abilities. While all of these arguments are compelling and important, with one exception, they all focus on the predictor side, meaning cognitive ability. Only the compatibility principle also integrates the criterion side. In the case of scholastic performance, especially when operationalized via grades, it seems worthwhile though to consider both the criterion and the predictor side.

1.2. Considering the Criterion—Specific Ability Relations

One of the more obvious problems with grades is criterion contamination and deficiency [25,38]. Grades can be derived from a variety of different exam forms: written tests, oral tests, or active participation to name just a few. Even when restricting research to written tests only, there are tests that are more objective (e.g., math exams) and tests that are less objective (e.g., essays) in a psychometrical sense. Thus, grades can be contaminated, which means that the variance of grades might in part be due to aspects actually not reflecting scholastic performance e.g., gender [42]. Criterion contamination could also mean that some of the criterion variance is actually not due to differences related to the predictor side. Considering that scholastic performance requires a multitude of abilities, traits, and skills [7], it is absolutely reasonable to assume that cognitive abilities will not be related to all psychological processes contributing to scholastic performance. In that sense, grades are contaminated with variance unrelated to cognitive abilities. We will come back to this notion later on.

On the other hand, cognitive abilities encompass such a broad spectrum of different processes, e.g., [31,43], that it is unlikely that school grades are influenced by all of these processes. This in turn can be regarded as a criterion deficiency. Unfortunately, considering contamination and deficiency has so far only been used to explain lower test criterion correlations in general. Thus, to revive specific abilities as predictors, these ideas need to be considered in a new way. We will do this here by connecting them with other influences on test-criterion correlations.

Variance decomposition and compatibility. Above, we have already mentioned one such influence: the compatibility aspect. So far, we have only looked at it in terms of level of symmetry or specific context. Unfortunately, it is impossible and maybe not even desirable to change grading to be better compatible with ability tests. There is, however, also a modeling perspective. Most of the research on intelligence and scholastic performance uses an average of grades in which each grade contributes equally. This is especially puzzling as research shows that the relation between grades and intelligence varies with subject [16]. Thus, when a trivial scoring function like the average is used, the variance shared by all grades is most likely being maximized due to the variance sum law (see Equation (1)). This is similar to a g-factor score, which maximizes the shared variance of the used ability tests. Clearly, this might favor the g-factor as predictor. However, even in studies where latent variables are used to decompose variance, specific abilities often do not contribute to performance. The alleged advantage of latent variable modeling is that each indicator of a reflective latent variable only contributes with the variance actually reflective of this variable, thereby decomposing the indicator variance into its constituents. The latent variable embodies shared variance and the residuals of the indicators specific variance. Deary et al. [44] used such latent variable modeling to estimate the true score correlation between scholastic performance and g (which was 0.81). However, this model would also have allowed testing for specific relations between residuals on both sides. This means that residuals of specific abilities (after controlling for g) could have been correlated with residuals of specific subject performance (after controlling for GPA). If such model modifications were to achieve a better model fit, it would show that specific ability test scores do in fact contain relevant variance. The reported model fit (CFI = 0.92) suggests room for model improvement [45,46]. Following up on this idea seems promising. However, this only makes sense with data that allow for modeling specific abilities such as latent variables, which means that item level information would be required. Unfortunately, the data set provided for analyses for all papers published in this special issue did not contain such fine-grained data. Thus, we will not report our findings here, but will provide details in material provided on the OSF link to this paper.[1] We report there how, by using variance decomposition based on structural equation modeling, we aimed at identifying specific relations, which might be blurred when using test scores or grades comprising different variance sources. In that sense, the relations between the residual factors were meant to have better compatibility and thus better chances of finding optimal correlations [39].

Nonlinear relations between cognitive ability and school performance. Another idea, which can be pursued with the current data, regards the nature of the relation between predictor and grade. As is typical in psychology, prior research almost exclusively used correlations and regressions, thereby assuming linear relations between predictors (abilities) and criteria (scholastic performance). However, following up this line of thinking would mean that more intelligence always yields better performance. This idea also means that the relation between ability and performance is assumed to be consistent across all levels of the predictor and criterion. Psychologically, this would mean that ability always contributes in the same way to performance. We have already pointed out above that scholastic

---

[1] The OSF link to this paper is: https://osf.io/g69ke/?view_only=9e35c20578904c37a418a7d03218dbff. Here, you can find the R code for these analyses, the data set, as well as further analyses mentioned.

performance is made up of a multitude of psychological processes. For example, when learning about linear algebra, it is certainly important to bring fluid and crystallized abilities along to understand the topic. At the same time, research shows that acquiring knowledge also benefits from being open to new stimuli and being interested in them [47], having a mastery oriented learning style [7], and a specific motivational structure [21,22]. Each of these traits points towards specific processes. Some of these are about allocating energy to learning and others are more about the persistence with which goals are pursued. Importantly, all of these contribute to scholastic performance incrementally to g. Coming back to the notion of criterion contamination, these relations can be considered contamination from the perspective of cognitive abilities as predictors. Thus, the changing importance of other predictors could be one mechanism causing curvilinear relations between ability and performance. Thus, for easy or moderately difficult tasks, cognitive ability could be relevant only to get a first understanding while motivation and learning style might be more important to obtain excellent results. For more complex tasks, it could be that differences in intelligence play out especially in the upper performance regions where rote learning and motivation alone are no longer sufficient. Consequently, it is reasonable to assume that believing in a linear world is highly problematic. Instead, it seems more than justified to also consider curvilinear relations. Before further discussing aspects of curvilinear relations, we want to introduce a second, and related mechanism which would lead to curvilinear effects, the ability differentiation hypothesis.

1.3. Considering the Predictor—Ability Differentiation Hypothesis

Spearman [26] is often credited for introducing the idea of differentiation within the structure of cognitive abilities across different ability levels [27]. Spearman, in his famous two factor theory, assumed that underlying all cognitive tasks is a general factor which is then complemented by a specific ability. Spearman also assumed that the role of this g-factor and the respective specific ability might differ across ability levels (He assumed a similar mechanism across age, which has found little empirical support though [48,49]). The core idea of this so-called ability differentiation hypothesis is that the role of the g-factor varies across different ability levels. In that sense, g can be seen as some kind of fuel for all specific abilities. Consequently, if the amount of fuel and in psychological terms, if central processes are limited, all other processes relying on this capacity will also be limited [50]. Higher ability groups in turn have more fuel and thus fewer limits on general capacity. Thus, specific abilities can play a more important role. Deary et al. [51] reasoned that only sufficient g would provide the foundation for applying specific abilities. As one consequence, the g factor has more saturation in lower ability groups. Using moderated factor analysis, such an effect could be confirmed in large and heterogeneous samples [48,49]. Moreover, there is also meta-analytical support for the notion of ability differentiation [52]. Importantly, this also bears consequences for the current research project. If we consider that sufficient g provides the foundation to apply specific abilities, we could expect that the relation between specific abilities and cognitive tasks cannot be linear. Only with increasing capacity with regards to g would specific abilities have sufficient fuel to influence task success. At the same time, higher g-factor levels are very likely to go along with higher scores on specific ability tests. Now, if we consider what we just pointed out above, which is the notion that tasks might require cognitive abilities depending on their level of complexity, we could reason that these effects can only be realized by students with sufficient g. Importantly, this would also lead to curvilinear relations between specific abilities and grades. To give a hypothetical example, in order to understand the mechanisms of linear algebra, numerical abilities might be needed in addition to g to master the basic performance level. In order to solve more complex tasks, often vested in short texts, verbal abilities might come into play and be even more important. As a consequence, the relation between numerical ability and performance would be stronger for grades reflecting low to moderate performance. Verbal abilities in turn might have stronger relations in the upper performance level. In each case, curvilinear relations would occur, suppositional on sufficient g-factor scores. Considering that samples like the one used here have undergone years of schooling and thus years of selection, it seems reasonable to assume that *g*-factor scores suffice. Considering the *g*-factor as the fuel or foundation for the specific abilities would also mean that it is predictive throughout the grade range, which would result in a more linear prediction. We want to stress here that this is purely speculation based on different theories; thus, we will not propose explicit hypotheses regarding the relation between specific abilities and specific subjects.

1.4. Curvilinear Relations

Curvilinear relations are comparable to a moderation effect. Whereas a moderation means that the slope representing the relation between two variables is influenced by a third variable, a curvilinear relation means that the slope is influenced by the level of one of the variables [53]. In that sense, the variable itself is the moderator. For the present research question, the relation between cognitive abilities and grades, this would mean that this relation depends on the level of the predictor. In other words, increments in ability are no longer contributing in the same way as before. Two general kinds of such curvilinear relations are reasonable when looking at the relation between cognitive ability and grades (see Figure 1). The first kind (see the left-hand side of Figure 1) would assume a negatively accelerated relation. This means that the relation between grades and ability is more pronounced in the lower ability regions. Importantly, the relation could be positive or negative in general. Moreover, it is also possible that the relation actually reverses at a certain point. A classical example for such a relation is the Yerkes–Dodson law [54]. A more relevant and more recent example can be found in a study by Antonakis et al. [55]. Those authors reported an inverted u shape relation between cognitive ability (measured with the Wonderlic test [56]) and perceived leadership behavior. Considering the relation between cognitive ability and grades, it seems unlikely that higher ability could actually decrease performance. However, it seems reasonable to assume that, from a certain point on, the impact of cognitive ability on performance might weaken or reach a plateau. An example for such a relation can be found in the study by Ganzach et al. [57]. Those authors could show that the relation between general mental ability and pay follows a curvilinear trend. For grades, this would mean that being brighter only gets you part of the way, which is one of our key arguments explained above. Afterwards, other aspects might be more important for achieving good grades. In that sense, grades would be contaminated as explained above.

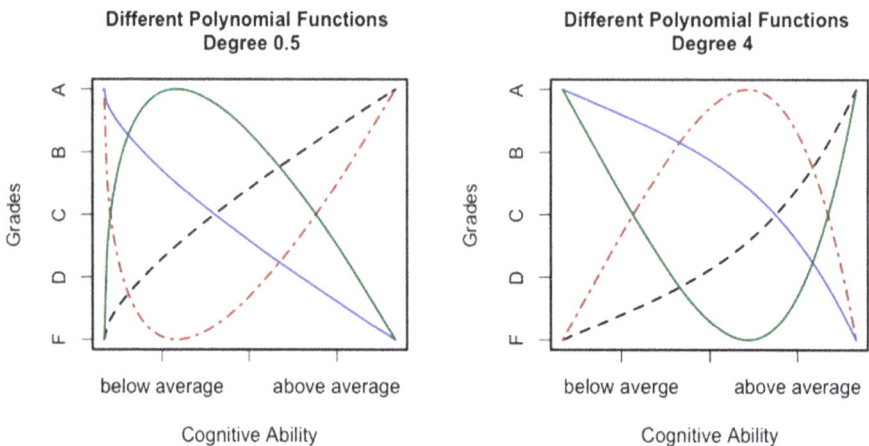

Figure 1. Hypothetical examples for curvilinear relations between cognitive ability and scholastic performance.

On the right side of Figure 1, a positively accelerated relation is depicted. The general idea here is that the relation between ability and performance starts out weak and then increases with increasing ability. As before, a reversal in the relation is also possible. Such a relation signifies the idea that cognitive abilities become important only at a higher level of ability and likewise when it is about better grades. This idea is in line with the ability differentiation hypothesis. This hypothesis assumes that specific abilities are more important at higher *g* levels. Here, it is important to note that *g* and the specific abilities are positively correlated. Thus, it is reasonable to assume that higher levels for specific abilities go along with higher *g* levels. For grades, this could mean that, due to having fewer limits with regards to general processes [50], specific abilities are able to exert their influence without restrictions. Especially for exams requiring solving complex problems, this should be advantageous, leading to better grades. Thus, we would expect stronger relations in the upper specific ability levels.

The different functions depicted in Figure 1 all have in common that the relation between ability and grades is not linear, or in other words, ability does not contribute equally across the whole ability range. We have argued above that this might be due to other predictor–performance relations also influencing performance. Importantly, these other relations might include subject specific aspects (e.g., the teacher or difficulty of exams). This can be explained with trait activation theory [58], which assumes that differences due to a trait manifest depend on the situation. Amongst other ideas, trait activation theory proposes the existence of constraints and distracters, which are situational features that make the manifestation of a trait less likely [59]. Such constraints and distracters might differ across subjects, which means that they would not contribute to the correlation between grades in all cases. Thus, when averaging across subjects, the specifics that led to a changing impact of ability will become relatively less important. This is due to the fact that adding variances also means to add the correlation between the summands:

$$\text{Variance Sum Law}: \sigma^2_{x\pm y} = \sigma^2_x + \sigma^2_y \pm 2\rho_{xy}\sigma_x\sigma_y. \tag{1}$$

In Equation (1), ρ equals the population estimate of the correlation and σ represents the population estimate of the standard evaluation. Thus, as mentioned before, it is vital to establish an equal level of symmetry. Therefore, we will analyze the impact of cognitive abilities on grades separately for each school subject.

It is now feasible to relate these statistical ideas to the ideas of criterion contamination and deficiency, as well as to the ability differentiation hypothesis. The first mechanism, suggested above, is based on criterion deficiency and puts forward the idea that specific abilities are more or less important at different grade levels. At other grade levels, the psychological processes underlying those specific abilities are less relevant and the grade is deficient in the sense that its variance is not due to the variance reflecting the specific ability. The variance is also contaminated because it contains the influences of other, most likely non-cognitive, traits. The second mechanism refers to ability differentiation and assumes that specific-abilities can only exert their influence at higher ability levels.

Another open question, however, is what specific kind of curvilinear relation to assume.

1.5. Modeling Curvilinear Effects

When it comes to modeling curvilinear effects, quadratic functions [60] seem to dominate psychological literature. While this kind of relation is intuitive, the modeling also comes along with a number of problems. On the very top of the problem list probably is the need for large samples due to lower power to detect such curvilinear effects [61]. Another issue is the threat of exploiting common method bias. This threat, however, has been refuted by Siemsen et al. [62]. One of the more severe criticisms is that a quadratic relation just is one out of many possible curvilinear relations [63]. Finally, it has recently been suggested that exploring the assumption of a simple quadratic relation (u or inverse u-shape) with linear regressions can be misleading [64]. Here, we will try to use a different statistical approach.

From a theoretical point of view, the idea of a changing relation between ability and grades might intuitively best be captured by a quadratic function. However, there is no convincing argument that a different curvilinear function would not be even better suited. In general, such functions are called polynomial functions. The term with the highest power (exponent) determines the degree of the polynomial. According to Cortina [53], it is vital to include nonlinear as well as linear terms. Thus, a simple function assuming only one predictor and the corresponding linear and curvilinear terms would be:

$$y_i = x_i + x_i^p + \varepsilon_i. \tag{2}$$

In this equation, x represents the predictor and y the criterion value for person I; p represents the degree of the polynomial. The last term reflects an individual prediction error (ε). It would be easy to look at the relation between ability and grades only with such an equation and only with one value for p (e.g., with $p = 2$). However, it seems much more promising to test several possible values for p and to select the best fitting out of all models. In machine learning, the use of complex algorithms to model relations is very common [65]. In that sense, multiple models with different values for the parameters are tested and a best fitting model is selected. This selection is then validated using different approaches. The field of psychology has been rather reluctant to embrace the chances that machine learning offers [66], the needed sample size probably ranging amongst the most important barriers. However, Yarkoni and Westfall [67] just recently propagated the use of machine learning in psychology, especially when aiming at prediction (also see [68] for an applied example). Considering the relation between grades and ability and its intricate complexities, machine learning seems like a promising avenue. While we applaud the recommendation to use machine learning in general, we will not apply complex algorithms like support vector machines or deep neural networks here for two reasons. The first reason is a statistical one. Machine learning results are prone to overfitting, which means that the complex algorithms find relations that are hard to replicate. Typically, this is dealt with during the validation by approaches in which data are split several times or hold-out samples are used. We will also use this approach here but still make a note of the relatively small sample size. The second reason is a more psychological one. Machine learning is often criticized as yielding black box algorithms that cannot be understood. While this might be true for very complex approaches, less complex approaches yield results that still can be interpreted straightforwardly. One such approach very useful for modeling curvilinear relations are complex polynomial functions [63]. The idea is to test different possibilities for p and then selecting the function yielding the best result. This function can then also be used to interpret the underlying processes. Clearly, this is a totally exploratory approach. Thus, the results should be considered as possibilities or hypotheses. The need for independent replications is especially high here.

In general, a polynomial function with linear and nonlinear terms and several predictors is:

$$y_i = \beta_0 + \beta_1 x_{i,1} + \beta_{11} x_{i,1}^{p_1} + \beta_2 x_{i,2} + \beta_{22} x_{i,2}^{p_2} + \cdots + \beta_q x_{i,q} + \beta_{qq} x_{i,q}^{p_q} + \varepsilon_i, i = 1 \ldots n q = 1 \ldots k \tag{3}$$

As before, x reflects the predictor and y the criterion values for person i. The second index, q, refers to the number of the predictor. In our case, when using specific abilities, we will have three different predictors. The power p reflects the degree of the polynomial. The index for each of these p values reflects the idea that the degrees of the polynomials can vary across predictors. In the current example, this would mean that the type of curvilinear relation between each specific ability test score and grades is not fixed but can be different. Finally, the impact of each term on the criterion is reflected in the regression weight β.

1.6. Summary and Aims of the Study

Considering the importance of school grades for success in later life, identifying the predictors of scholastic performance and shedding light onto the nature of these specific relations is an important goal. With regards to cognitive abilities as predictors, prior research has often emphasized the importance of *g* and questioned the use of specific cognitive abilities. The current paper proposes the idea of curvilinear relations between specific abilities and grades based on the idea of criterion contamination and deficiency as well as on the ability differentiation hypothesis. To be more precise, we propose that performance on different levels, meaning different grades, requires different abilities. For example, whereas numeric abilities might be necessary to master the basics of a new mathematical technique, verbal abilities might come into play at higher levels. Moreover, at specific levels of performance, other traits, for example, personality, interests, and motivation, might be more decisive, thereby causing a change in the impact of ability. Another mechanism could be that, due to ability differentiation, specific abilities can only exert their impact on performance in higher ability ranges, thereby also resulting in better grades. Considering Spearman's ideas about the *g*-factor, an impact of these mechanisms on the relation between grades and the *g*-factor is less likely. Thus, the test-criterion relations of specific abilities should profit more from adding curvilinear terms.

The current paper aims at testing the idea of curvilinear relations between specific abilities and grades. To this end, we will use an easy machine learning approach based on polynomial regressions. The advantage of such an approach is that more complex relations than just quadratic relations can be tested as well. This procedure must be considered data driven and exploratory. Thus, we will not propose any specific hypotheses and content ourselves with finding the best models for each school subject and then coming up with post hoc hypotheses as to the nature of the effects. We hope that these hypotheses as well as the statistical approach in general can inspire future research.

2. Methods

2.1. Sample, Measures, and Procedure

The data set used here is the one provided by the guest-editors of this special issue. It contains a sample of $n = 219$ students ($n = 117$ females) with a mean age of 16.03 ($SD = 1.49$). Each student value on the specific ability tests Unfolding, Analogies, and Number Series was reported. Unfolding is a figural test from the Wilde-Intelligence Test 2 [69]. Both of the other tests are from the same test battery. Analogies is a verbal analogy test and number series a complex test, which is why it is still considered an indicator of reasoning. Additionally, grades in math, German, English, and physical education (sports) were provided. The grades were coded with a range from 1 to 6 (from 1 = insufficient, 2 = with deficits, 3 = sufficient, 4 = satisfactory, 5 = good, 6 = very good). No further details were provided. Descriptive statistics as well as correlations between all variables can be found in Table 1.

Table 1. Means, standard deviations, and correlations with confidence intervals.

Variable	M	SD	1	2	3	4	5	6	7	8	9	10	11
1. Age	16.03	1.49											
2. Unfolding	9.31	4.26	0.12 [−0.01, 0.25]										
3. Unfolding scaled	3.00	1.00	0.12 [−0.01, 0.25]	1.00 ** [1.00, 1.00]									
4. Analogies	8.21	3.80	0.31 ** [0.19, 0.43]	0.33 ** [0.21, 0.44]	0.33 ** [0.21, 0.44]								
5. Analogies scaled	3.00	1.00	0.31 ** [0.19, 0.43]	0.33 ** [0.21, 0.44]	0.33 ** [0.21, 0.44]	1.00 ** [1.00, 1.00]							
6. Number Series	8.26	4.01	0.21 ** [0.08, 0.33]	0.39 ** [0.27, 0.50]	0.39 ** [0.27, 0.50]	0.39 ** [0.27, 0.50]	0.39 ** [0.27, 0.50]						
7. Number Series scaled	3.00	1.00	0.21 ** [0.08, 0.33]	0.39 ** [0.27, 0.50]	0.39 ** [0.27, 0.50]	0.39 ** [0.27, 0.50]	0.39 ** [0.27, 0.50]	10.00 ** [1.00, 1.00]					
8. Factor Score (g)	−0.00	0.81	0.28 ** [0.15, 0.39]	0.71 ** [0.64, 0.77]	0.71 ** [0.64, 0.77]	0.72 ** [0.64, 0.77]	0.72 ** [0.64, 0.77]	0.85 ** [0.80, 0.88]	0.85 ** [0.80, 0.88]				
9. Factor Score (g) scaled	3.00	1.00	0.28 ** [0.15, 0.39]	0.71 ** [0.64, 0.77]	0.71 ** [0.64, 0.77]	0.72 ** [0.64, 0.77]	0.72 ** [0.64, 0.77]	0.85 ** [0.80, 0.88]	0.85 ** [0.80, 0.88]	1.00 ** [1.00, 1.00]			
10. Grade German	3.91	0.94	0.23 ** [0.10, 0.35]	0.22 ** [0.09, 0.34]	0.22 ** [0.09, 0.34]	0.24 ** [0.11, 0.36]	0.24 ** [0.11, 0.36]	0.19 ** [0.06, 0.32]	0.19 ** [0.06, 0.32]	0.28 ** [0.15, 0.40]	0.28 ** [0.15, 0.40]		
11. Grade English	3.74	0.94	0.19 ** [0.06, 0.32]	0.13 [−0.00, 0.26]	0.13 [−0.00, 0.26]	0.27 ** [0.15, 0.39]	0.27 ** [0.15, 0.39]	0.22 ** [0.09, 0.34]	0.22 ** [0.09, 0.34]	0.27 ** [0.14, 0.39]	0.27 ** [0.14, 0.39]	0.54 ** [0.44, 0.63]	
12. Grade Sports	5.05	0.72	−0.01 [−0.15, 0.12]	−0.01 [−0.14, 0.13]	−0.01 [−0.14, 0.13]	0.10 [−0.04, 0.22]	0.10 [−0.04, 0.22]	0.03 [−0.11, 0.16]	0.03 [−0.11, 0.16]	0.05 [−0.09, 0.18]	0.05 [−0.09, 0.18]	0.16 * [0.02, 0.28]	0.11 [−0.02, 0.24]

Note. * indicates $p < 0.05$; ** indicates $p < 0.01$. M and SD are used to represent mean and standard deviation, respectively. Values in square brackets indicate the 95% confidence interval for each correlation. The confidence interval is a plausible range of population correlations that could have caused the sample correlation [70].

2.2. Statistical Analyses

All analyses were conducted in R [71] using RStudio [72] and the packages *psych* [73], *lm.beta* [74], *knitr* [75], *apaTables* [76], *caret* [77], *tidyverse* [78], and *readr* [79]. In order to prepare the data, we first estimated a *g* score for each person by extracting a factor score on the first unrotated factor of a factor analysis (principal axis factoring) of the three specific ability tests. The loadings were 0.57 (Unfolding), 0.58 (Analogies), and 0.68 (Number Series). The eigenvalue was 1.13 and the factor explained 38 percent of the variance. In a next step, we scaled the predictors (i.e., the three specific ability tests as well as the factor score) to use them in the polynomial regressions [56]. To avoid nonessential collinearity resulting from scaling [80] and, in order to ease interpretation, we centered the scores. We also followed advice form machine learning literature and additionally standardized the scores [80]. We used a value of three as a center and a variance of one. The value of three was chosen to avoid negative values, which are not defined in some polynomials (e.g., $p = 0.5$). Moreover, the grade scale theoretically ranges from 1 to 5, which makes 3 the theoretical mean value.

In a next analytical step, we simply ran two multiple linear regressions for each school subject. Within the first regression, we used the factor score representing *g* as independent variable. In the second regression, the three specific ability test scores served as independent variables. These analyses were conducted as a kind of baseline for the following analyses.

We then ran two series of polynomial regressions for each school subject. In the first series, we used the factor score as a proxy for *g* as predictor. In the other series, we used the three specific ability test scores. In order to avoid collinearity, we did not include the *g*-factor score in the specific ability models. We also refrained from residualizing the *g*-factor score in order to keep interpretability straightforward. In order to compare the *g*-factor models with the specific ability models, we compared the prediction accuracy and the adjusted R^2s. While the prediction accuracy tells us something about the utility of the model in general, the R^2 helps to gauge the effect size. In a regression analysis, the variance shared by all predictors with the criterion is reflected in R^2. Thus, larger values for the specific ability models would imply an additional impact of the specific ability test scores compared to the *g*-factor only models. In each series, we ran a sequence for *p* starting at a value of 0 to a value of 5 in steps of 0.5. We left out the value of 1 because it would lead to collapsing the terms meant to represent linear and nonlinear aspects. We did allow the *p*-values to vary for each predictor (resulting in 8000 models for each grade and predicted by the specific abilities). Thus, the functions were:

$$grade = \beta_0 + \beta_1 \cdot g + \beta_{11} \cdot g^p + \varepsilon, \tag{4}$$

for the *g*-factor score and:

$$grade = \beta_0 + \beta_1 \cdot Unfolding + \beta_{11} \cdot Unfolding^{p_1} + \beta_2 \cdot Analogies + \beta_{21} \cdot Analogies^{p_2} + \\ \beta_3 \cdot Number\ Series + \beta_{31} \cdot Number\ Series^{p_3} + \varepsilon \tag{5}$$

for the specific abilities, respectively. In order to minimize the risk of overfitting, we used a leave-one-out technique. In particular, we ran each possible model on the whole data set, leaving out one person. The resulting function was used to predict the value of this left out person. This was repeated for every person in the data set. The absolute values of the differences between the actually observed grades and the predicted values were then computed, yielding 219 deviations. These values followed a skewed distribution (many small deviations, few large ones), which is why we decided to use the median and not the mean of these values. This median was used as an estimate of the prediction accuracy (labeled RMSE (root mean square error) following the tradition in the literature) and the model with the lowest value was selected. In that sense, the selected model is the one yielding the lowest discrepancy between the observed and the model implied grade. Using this approach, we selected the best model for each grade and each predictor combination (i.e., *g*-factor score vs. specific ability test scores). In order to decide whether the models with the specific ability test scores yielded larger effect sizes for a specific grade, we also compared the respective adjusted R^2s. For each selected model, we used the R^2 estimated using the selected function and data from the complete sample.

To get a better idea of the function behind the models for the specific abilities, we plotted the functions varying each predictor and holding the other predictors constant at the centered mean value. Thus, for each grade and the specific ability test score models, three functions were plotted. All R codes and results (as html) can be found in the OSF material.[2]

3. Results

3.1. Multiple Linear Regressions

Table 2 contains the results for the linear regressions using the *g*-factor score as independent variable. It can be seen that the models yield moderate (German and English) to strong relations (math) with the exception of sports. Accordingly, the regression weights were significant with the exception of sports. Table 3 contains the findings obtained when using scores for the three specific abilities as predictors. While the R^2's are descriptively larger for the models with the specific ability test scores, the adjusted R^2's are mostly smaller. The exception here is English, where specific ability test scores achieve a larger R^2. However, the difference is only 0.7 percent. Again, sports could not be predicted at all. The regression weights for the Analogies score were significant for math, German, and English. The Unfolding and Number Series scores only predicted math grades. Thus, all in all, the classical approach does not yield findings in support of using specific ability test scores. Moreover, at this point, we decided to drop the sports grade from further analyses.

Table 2. Regression results using the different grades as criteria and the factor score (*g*) as predictor.

Subject	Predictor	*b*	*b* 95% CI [*LL, UL*]	*β*	*β* 95% CI [*LL, UL*]	*r*	R^2	*Adj. R^2*
Math								
	Factor Score (*g*)	0.44 **	[0.32, 0.56]	0.44	[0.32, 0.56]	0.44 **		
							R^2 = 0.198 ** 95% CI [0.11, 0.29]	0.194
German								
	Factor Score (*g*)	0.28 **	[0.15, 0.41]	0.28	[0.15, 0.41]	0.28 **		
							R^2 = 0.077 ** 95% CI [0.02, 0.15]	0.073
English								
	Factor Score (*g*)	0.27 **	[0.14, 0.40]	0.27	[0.14, 0.40]	0.27 **		
							R^2 = 0.074 ** 95% CI [0.02, 0.15]	0.070
Sports								
	Factor Score (*g*)	0.05	[−0.09, 0.18]	0.05	[−0.09, 0.18]	0.05		
							R^2 = 0.002 95% CI [0.00, 0.03]	−0.002

Note. * indicates $p < 0.05$; ** indicates $p < 0.01$. A significant *b*-weight indicates the *β*-weight and semi-partial correlation are also significant. *b* represents unstandardized regression weights; *β* indicates the standardized regression weights; *r* represents the zero-order correlation. *LL* and *UL* indicate the lower and upper limits of a confidence interval, respectively. *Adj.* R^2 represents the amount of explained variance adjusted for sample size and number of predictors.

---

[2] The OSF link to this paper is: https://osf.io/g69ke/?view_only=9e35c20578904c37a418a7d03218dbff. Here, you can find the R code for these analyses, the data set, as well as further analyses mentioned.

Table 3. Regression results using the different grades as criteria and the specific abilities as predictors.

Subject	Predictor	*b*	*b* 95% CI [LL, UL]	*β*	*β* 95% CI [LL, UL]	*sr²*	*sr²* 95% CI [LL, UL]	*r*	*R²*	*Adj. R²*
Math										
	Unfolding	0.15 *	[0.02, 0.28]	0.15	[0.02, 0.28]	0.02	[−0.01, 0.05]	0.31 **		
	Analogies	0.22 **	[0.08, 0.35]	0.22	[0.08, 0.35]	0.04	[−0.01, 0.08]	0.35 **		
	Number Series	0.22 **	[0.08, 0.35]	0.22	[0.08, 0.35]	0.04	[−0.01, 0.08]	0.36 **		
									R^2 = 0.200 ** 95% CI [0.11, 0.28]	0.189
German										
	Unfolding	0.14	[−0.01, 0.28]	0.14	[−0.01, 0.28]	0.01	[−0.02, 0.05]	0.22 **		
	Analogies	0.16 *	[0.02, 0.31]	0.16	[0.02, 0.31]	0.02	[−0.02, 0.06]	0.24 **		
	Number Series	0.08	[−0.07, 0.22]	0.08	[−0.07, 0.22]	0.00	[−0.01, 0.02]	0.19 **		
									R^2 = 0.083 ** 95% CI [0.02, 0.15]	0.071
English										
	Unfolding	0.01	[−0.14, 0.15]	0.01	[−0.14, 0.15]	0.00	[−0.00, 0.00]	0.13		
	Analogies	0.22 **	[0.08, 0.36]	0.22	[0.08, 0.36]	0.04	[−0.01, 0.09]	0.27 **		
	Number Series	0.13	[−0.01, 0.28]	0.13	[−0.01, 0.28]	0.01	[−0.02, 0.04]	0.22 **		
									R^2 = 0.089 ** 95% CI [0.02, 0.16]	0.077
Sports										
	Unfolding	−0.04	[−0.19, 0.11]	−0.04	[−0.19, 0.11]	0.00	[−0.01, 0.01]	−0.01		
	Analogies	0.11	[−0.04, 0.26]	0.11	[−0.04, 0.26]	0.01	[−0.02, 0.04]	0.10		
	Number Series	−0.00	[−0.15, 0.15]	−0.00	[−0.15, 0.15]	0.00	[−0.00, 0.00]	0.03		
									R^2 = 0.011 95% CI [<0.01, 0.04]	−0.003

Note. * indicates $p < 0.05$; ** indicates $p < 0.01$. A significant *b*-weight indicates the *β*-weight and semi-partial correlation are also significant. *b* represents unstandardized regression weights; *β* indicates the standardized regression weights; sr^2 represents the semi-partial correlation squared; *r* represents the zero-order correlation. *LL* and *UL* indicate the lower and upper limits of a confidence interval, respectively. *Adj. R²* represents the amount of explained variance adjusted for sample size and number of predictors.

3.2. Selecting the Best Fitting Model

In the next step, we tested the different polynomial regression models, thereby testing curvilinear relations. Figure 2 contains the RMSEs for all models with the *g*-factor only and all models with the specific ability test scores as predictors in ascending order.

As can be seen, the values roughly range between 0.60 and 0.70. Thus, the differences between the models were not pronounced. Moreover, it can be seen that, while the model with linear terms only fit best whenever the *g*-factor score was used as a predictor, the models with specific ability test scores as predictor yielded the best results when assuming curvilinear relations. In order to exemplify the influence of changing from a linear to a curvilinear model, Figure 3 depicts the RMSEs for all models specified for each grade and in relation to the average polynomial degree as well as the actual number of polynomial terms. The different colors reflect the number of polynomial terms ranging from zero (linear model) to 3 (all specific ability test scores have a curvilinear relation with the grade). To simplify the figure, the actual polynomial degrees were averaged. Those values are used on the *x*-axis. The *y*-axis reflects the RMSE of each model. For example, the plot on the right contains all RMSEs for models with math grade as dependent and specific ability test scores as independent variables. It can be seen that the model with linear terms only (red dot) ranged in the middle. Thus, there were many curvilinear models better, but also many worse than the linear model for math as dependent variable. It can further be seen that the best models for math had two polynomial terms whose average degrees were below 2 (green dots). However, those models also belonged to the worst models for math, which indicates that the three specific ability test scores might have quite dissimilar relations with the grades. Regarding the other grades, the linear models never performed well.

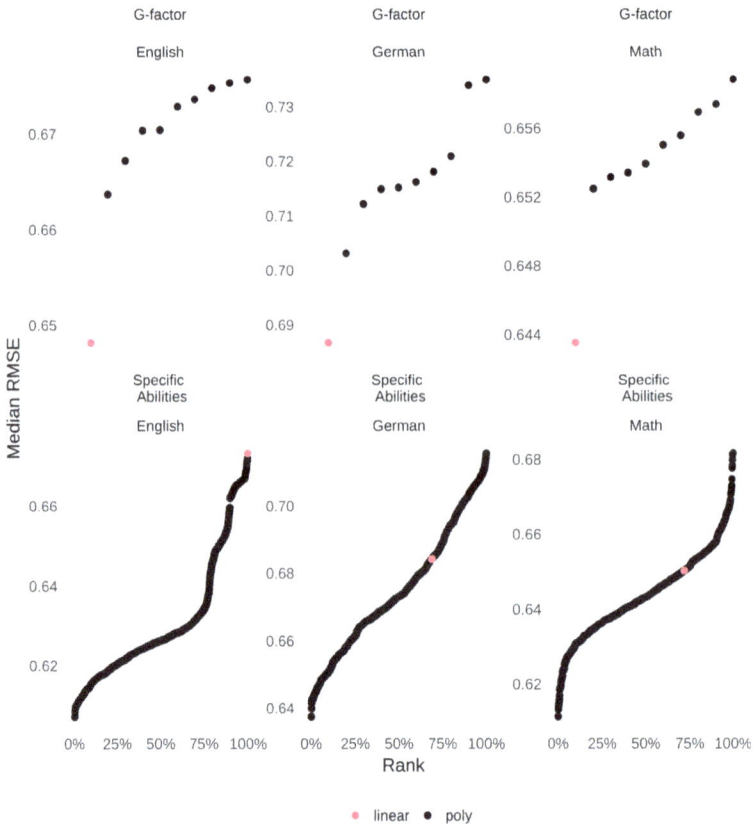

Figure 2. Ranked RMSEs for all models in ascending order. Percentiles on the *x*-axis. A red dot always represents the model with linear terms only.

The parameter estimates for the best models can be found in Table 4. For the *g*-factor models, this was the linear model in all cases. For the models with the specific ability test scores as predictors, the results were different. Here, the polynomial achieved more accurate predictions (lower average RMSEs) and we selected them as the best fitting models. Looking at the actual polynomial degrees shows that only the Unfolding and Analogies test scores had curvilinear relations with the grade in each school subject. The Number Series test score did not have a curvilinear relation with the math grade.

When comparing the *g*-factor only and specific ability test score models for each school subject, it can be seen that the models with the specific ability tests scores yielded a more accurate prediction (lower average RMSE) for all grades. Importantly, these advantages in accuracy, which might simply be due to the larger number of predictors, were also reflected with regards to the adjusted R^2s: models with the specific ability test scores and curvilinearity were better for all subjects. Referring to Gignac and Szodorai [81], the effects can be considered as small to medium (also see [82]). Comparing the differences with the differences between the adjusted R^2's from the linear regressions (see Tables 3 and 4) shows that the predictive power of the specific ability test scores profited relatively strongly, now yielding an advantage compared with the *g*-factor score models.

All in all, the results support the notion of curvilinear relations between specific cognitive ability test scores and grades.

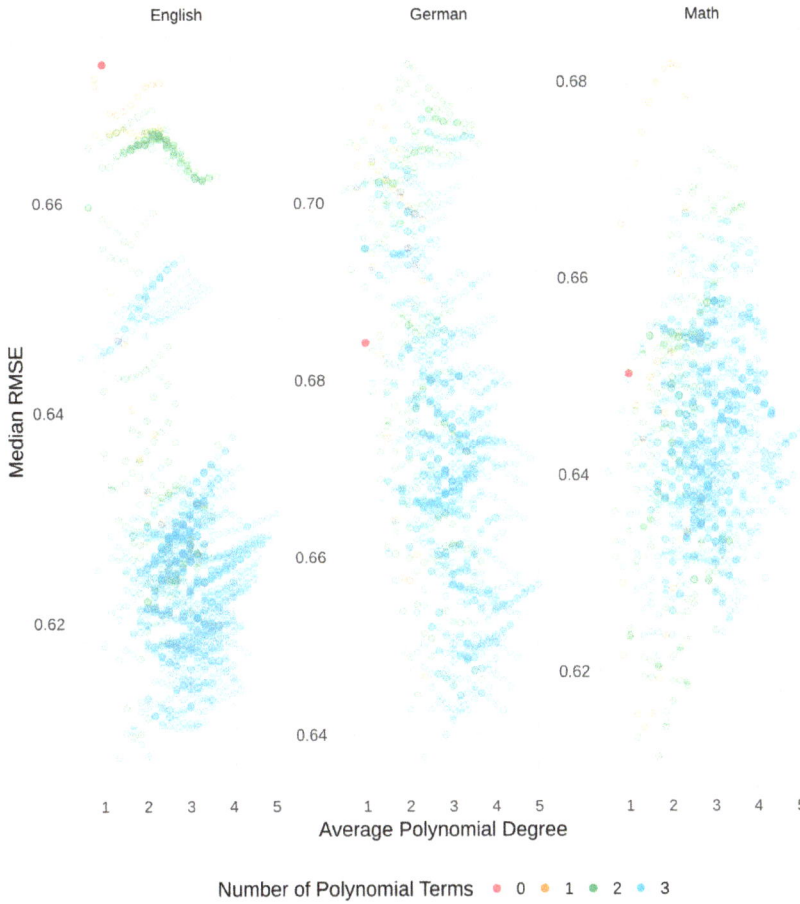

Figure 3. RMSEs for all models. The *x*-axis lists the average of the polynomial degrees (e.g., Unfolding^2, Analogies^3, NumberSeries^4 results in an *x*-value of [2 + 3 + 4]/3 = 3). The model with linear terms only is depicted in red.

Table 4. Summaries of the best fitting linear and polynomial equations.

Predictor	Criterion	Degree			Adjusted R^2	RMSE
g-factor						
	Math	1			0.194	0.644
	German	1			0.073	0.687
	English	1			0.070	0.648
Specific Ability Test Scores	**Unfolding**	**Analogies**	**Number Series**			
	Math	2	2	1	0.220	0.611
	German	3	0.5	0.5	0.083	0.637
	English	5	0.5	1.5	0.091	0.607

3.3. Exploring the Nature of the Curvilinear Relations

To explore the nature of the found relations, we plotted the best fitting models for all specific ability test score models and the curvilinear *g*-factor model. As could be seen in Table 4, the *g*-factor score always has a linear relation with the grade. The Number Series scores (blue line) also followed an almost linear relation. For Analogies scores (green line), the nature of the curve suggests an accelerating relation. This would mean that the captured ability has a stronger relation with performance for higher levels of this ability. This was especially pronounced for the math grade. Unfolding scores (orange line) had a curvilinear relation with all grades. In each case, its relation deteriorated around the mean level.

4. Discussion

The current paper addressed the issue of specific vs. general cognitive abilities by referring to three theoretical ideas. First, we emphasized the necessity to match predictor and criterion in terms of the level of abstraction (comparability principle). Second, we suggested two mechanisms, which would impact the form of the relation between specific ability test scores and grades. We referred to Brogden's [25] ideas of criterion contamination and deficiency to deduce a mechanism influencing the relation between specific ability test scores and performance. We assumed that the influence of specific abilities changes once other traits become more or less important for performance. The other, suggested mechanism, building on Spearman's ability differentiation hypothesis, was the idea that specific abilities exert their influence only when sufficient levels are reached. Both mechanisms would yield nonlinear relations between the specific abilities and scholastic performance. This was the third theoretical idea brought forward and tested here using the provided data set. Applying polynomial regressions, it was found that models containing linear and nonlinear terms outperform simple linear models when using specific ability test scores. Moreover, these models with specific ability tests were more accurate and better predictors of grades compared to models only containing a factor score reflecting *g*. Finally, the analyses showcase the utility of machine learning.

4.1. Specific Abilities and Scholastic Performance

As was reported before, using scores from specific ability tests to predict scholastic performance did not yield findings superior to using a *g*-factor as the only predictor when using multiple linear regressions. However, the picture changed, when polynomial regressions were used and thus when assuming curvilinear relations. In particular, while this did not change the predictive power of *g*, the findings for the specific ability tests were improved. In fact, the improvement was strong enough to tentatively state that the models outperformed both the linear models as well as the models only containing *g*. While this finding is interesting per se, it also bears some potential theoretical implications. Especially with regards to the scores obtained from the Unfolding and Analogies tests, the findings call for more specific hypotheses. Above, we have already stated that we will not make specific a priori hypotheses. Now that we know the results, we will suggest some post hoc explanations based on these findings. We want to emphasize that these explanations are totally data driven at this point.

Unfolding. The Unfolding test score showed the most interesting pattern. In a linear regression, it was only significant for the prediction of math. In the polynomial regressions, this was different. The plots in Figure 4 suggest that the ability measured is related to scholastic performance mainly in the below average ability range. What this means is that the ability measured becomes less important once a threshold is met. In other words, this ability would be a requisite for passing but would not suffice to excel. Looking at the relation from the perspective of the grades, the findings could also mean that, in order to achieve truly excellent grades, other traits are of more importance. In any case, it would be beneficial to have a better understanding of the test in question. Unfolding tests as the one used here typically measure spatial and reasoning abilities. It is often assumed that such tests are good predictors of fluid intelligence (gf) because of their relatively low demand for crystalized ability (e.g., knowledge of words or numbers). Taking this into account, it could be argued that the test is a good indicator of gf. It has to be noted though that we used only one indicator of this ability. Thus, the variance due to the specific ability might be confounded with variance due to the specific test tasks. However, if we accept that this one test could be an indicator of gf, it would mean that gf is a necessary condition to master math. However, it does not suffice to truly excel, at least in terms of school grades. As noted above, other traits such as personality, motives, or interests might be more relevant. For a large sample of Swedish recruits, Lindqvist and Vestman [83] analyzed the long-term importance of ability and personality with regards to job success. They reported that cognitive ability is especially important for the initial success, while personality was important for the long-term success. It is reasonable to assume that scholastic success follows similar patterns, specifically when it comes to specific abilities or even gf. Of course, we want to emphasize that these ideas are purely speculative and should be seen as hypotheses. Further research with independent data sets is necessary to gauge the sustainability of these thoughts.

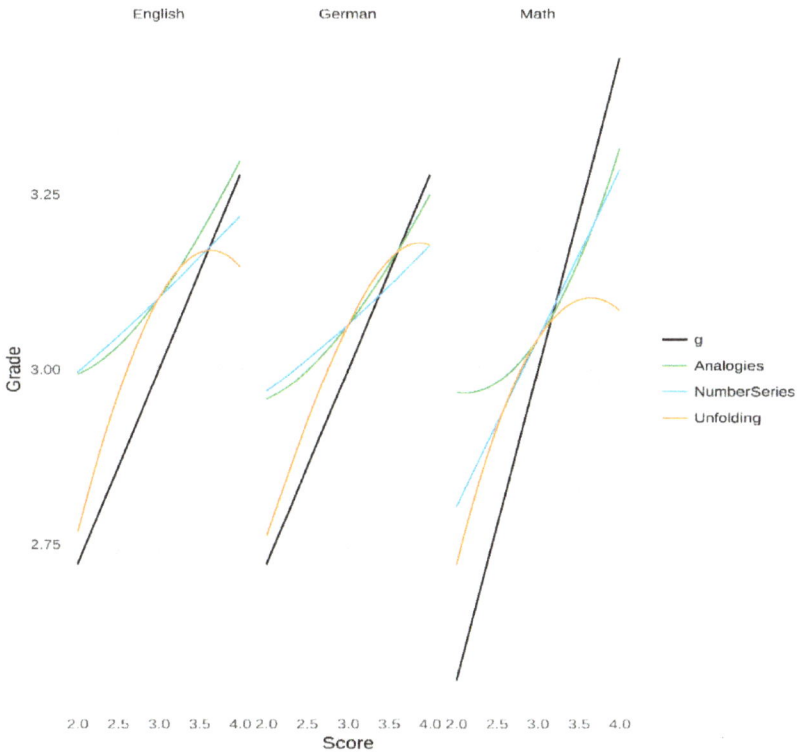

Figure 4. Relation between grades and ability test scores estimated from the selected models. In the case of several predictors, the levels for the respective other predictors were fixed at 3.

Analogies. Interestingly, a curvilinear relation between this ability and scholastic performance was especially pronounced in math. The analogies test used here requires a certain amount of vocabulary and reasoning. Vocabulary is a good indicator of crystallized intelligence [84]. It is reasonable to assume that the specific ability measured here helps to analyze and comprehend complex texts. In school, such texts become more and more regular even in math exams once the students enter higher grades. Thus, as argued above, it might be possible that, in order to achieve excellent grades in math, it does not suffice to understand the logic behind the analyses. It is also important to comprehend the texts within books and, maybe even more importantly, within exams [85]. This would explain why higher scores in the analogies tests are predictive of better grades.

Combining this idea with the idea of Unfolding being a specific ability test from the realm of gf tests, the current findings suggest that fluid ability might help to achieve moderate grades in math. However, in order to achieve excellent grades, above average verbal abilities might be needed.

Future research could test these ideas by either analyzing or manipulating exams with regards to their reliance on text-based tasks. This finding is also in line with the mechanism derived from Spearman's ability differentiation hypothesis. The current results show that the relation between the Analogies test scores and math performance becomes stronger in the upper regions of the ability.

On the other hand, and also with regards to Unfolding scores, the idea of grades being contaminated with the influence of other traits (e.g., interests) could be behind the observed curvilinear pattern. The results also support the notion that different specific abilities are relevant for different grade levels. It has to be noted that, given the nature of the data used, we cannot test these mechanisms directly, nor can we draw actual causal interpretations. Nevertheless, the findings are encouraging and should inspire future research to apply similar statistical approaches to longitudinal data, ideally comprising a wide range of abilities and traits.

4.2. Machine Learning

In recent years, the application of machine learning algorithms has attracted more and more attention in psychology [86–88]. Here, we also use a machine learning approach but refer to much simpler algorithms. Still, the findings are encouraging and support the notion of furthering scientific knowledge using such complex methods. Importantly this study shows that the results and algorithms must not remain black boxes. Admittedly, applying more complex approaches like deep neural networks or support vector machines might prove even more fruitful with regards to optimizing prediction. However, in some cases, prediction alone does not suffice. Especially when it comes to predictors of scholastic performance, it seems vital to understand their relation to performance. The current analyses show that it is possible to take advantage of machine learning without giving up the possibility to derive at conclusions about possible mechanisms. Thus, we further encourage using machine learning approaches, including validation strategies, in psychological research.

4.3. Limitations and Outlook

The generalizability of the reported findings suffers from some limitations. Most obvious is the small sample size and the limited number of variables at hand. However, this article being part of a special issue in which everyone used the same data set outweighs this potentially damaging limitation. Due to the fact that no item level information was available, a possible alternative explanation can not be ruled out. We have emphasized above that the relation between performance and ability might not be the same across all ability levels. It is also possible that the actual ability captured within the test is not the same across score levels. This would mean that the kind of construct measured differs with differing test scores. This could also yield curvilinear relations. Measurement invariance tests would be required to test whether the same ability is captured for all score levels. Again, this is an interesting idea for future research. Another limitation comes along with the machine learning approach. While we tried to take precautions in order to avoid overfitting, no real replication was possible based on this sample. Thus, generalizing the current findings should be avoided until replications support the notion of curvilinear relations. Finally, the current paper does not really capture specific abilities. Each specific ability mentioned is only measured with one test. These tests contain variance due to g, the specific ability, and measurement error, but also task specific variance. Moreover, the variance accounted for by the g-factor often is rather substantial [36]. While this further explains the rather modest increments in R^2, it also means that a strong test of the hypotheses stated above needs to operationalize each specific ability with more than one test. Related to this is a possible influence of measurement error. Typically, ability test scores are less reliable in the boundary areas. Within our analyses, this could have led to floor or ceiling effects, which in turn might also yield curvilinear relations. Especially for the Unfolding test score, this might be an alternative explanation as the form of the function does not seem to differ much across subjects. In order to rule this out, it is necessary to use tests matching the students' abilities. Adaptive tests might be a promising approach. Despite these shortcomings, we hope that the findings inspire such replication efforts.

5. Conclusions

The current paper started with the idea that the world is not linear. The analyses conducted support this notion with regards to the relation between specific cognitive abilities and scholastic performance. Based on Brogden's [25] ideas of criterion contamination and deficiency as well as Spearman's ability differentiation hypothesis, possible mechanisms causing curvilinear relations were suggested. Using the data provided by the guest editors, we tested this idea by utilizing polynomial regressions. The findings support the idea of nonlinear relations between specific abilities and scholastic performance. Based on these results, we suggest that some cognitive abilities might simply help to achieve a moderate level of performance while others are necessary to truly excel.

Author Contributions: M.Z. designed the research strategy. A.P. advised on machine learning specifics and created the respective R codes. M.Z. wrote the paper and A.P. commented.

Conflicts of Interest: The authors declare no conflict of interest.

References

1. Fleming, J. Who will succeed in college? When the sat predicts black students' performance. *Rev. Higher Educ.* **2002**, *25*, 281–296. [CrossRef]
2. Hoffman, J.L.; Lowitzki, K.E. Predicting college success with high school grades and test scores: Limitations for minority students. *Rev. Higher Educ.* **2005**, *28*, 455–474. [CrossRef]
3. Adams, S.J. Educational attainment and health: Evidence from a sample of older adults. *Educ. Econ.* **2002**, *10*, 97–109. [CrossRef]
4. French, M.T.; Homer, J.F.; Popovici, I.; Robins, P.K. What you do in high school matters: High school gpa, educational attainment, and labor market earnings as a young adult. *East. Econ. J.* **2015**, *41*, 370–386. [CrossRef]
5. Poropat, A.E. A meta-analysis of the five-factor model of personality and academic performance. *Psychol. Bull.* **2009**, *135*, 322–338. [CrossRef] [PubMed]
6. Di Fabio, A.; Busoni, L. Fluid intelligence, personality traits and scholastic success: Empirical evidence in a sample of italian high school students. *Personal. Individ. Differ.* **2007**, *43*, 2095–2104. [CrossRef]
7. Zhang, J.; Ziegler, M. How do the big five influence scholastic performance? A big five-narrow traits model or a double mediation model. *Learn. Individ. Differ.* **2016**, *50*, 93–102. [CrossRef]
8. Ziegler, M.; Knogler, M.; Bühner, M. Conscientiousness, achievement striving, and intelligence as performance predictors in a sample of german psychology students: Always a linear relationship? *Learn. Individ. Differ.* **2009**, *19*, 288–292. [CrossRef]
9. Kuncel, N.R.; Hezlett, S.A.; Ones, D.S. Academic performance, career potential, creativity, and job performance: Can one construct predict them all? *J. Personal. Soc. Psychol.* **2004**, *86*, 148–161. [CrossRef] [PubMed]
10. Schmidt, F.L.; Hunter, J.E. General mental ability in the world of work: Occupational attainment and job performance. *J. Personal. Soc. Psychol.* **2004**, *86*, 162–173. [CrossRef] [PubMed]
11. Schmidt, F.L.; Hunter, J.E. The validity and utility of selection methods in personnel psychology: Practical and theoretical implications of 85 years of research findings. *Psychol. Bull.* **1998**, *124*, 262–274. [CrossRef]
12. Gottfredson, L.S. Why g matters: The complexity of everyday life. *Intelligence* **1997**, *24*, 79–132. [CrossRef]
13. Gottfredson, L.S.; Deary, I.J. Intelligence predicts health and longevity, but why? *Curr. Direct. Psychol. Sci.* **2004**, *13*, 1–14. [CrossRef]
14. Coyle, T.R. Relations among general intelligence (g), aptitude tests, and GPA: Linear effects dominate. *Intelligence* **2015**, *53*, 16–22. [CrossRef]
15. Neisser, U.; Boodoo, G.; Bouchard, T.J.; Boykin, A.W.; Brody, N.; Ceci, S.J.; Halpern, D.F.; Loehlin, J.C.; Perloff, R.; Sternberg, R.J.; et al. Intelligence: Knowns and unknowns. *Am. Psychol.* **1996**, *51*, 77–101. [CrossRef]
16. Roth, B.; Becker, N.; Romeyke, S.; Schäfer, S.; Domnick, F.; Spinath, F.M. Intelligence and school grades: A meta-analysis. *Intelligence* **2015**, *53*, 118–137. [CrossRef]

17. Cucina, J.M.; Peyton, S.T.; Su, C.; Byle, K.A. Role of mental abilities and mental tests in explaining high-school grades. *Intelligence* **2016**, *54*, 90–104. [CrossRef]
18. McGrew, K.S. CHC theory and the human cognitive abilities project: Standing on the shoulders of the giants of psychometric intelligence research. *Intelligence* **2009**, *37*, 1–10. [CrossRef]
19. Schneider, W.J.; McGrew, K. The cattell-horn-carroll model of intelligence. In *Contemporary Intellectual Assessment: Theories, Tests, and Issues*; Flanagan, D.P., Harrison, P.L., Eds.; Guilford Press: New York, NY, USA, 2012; pp. 99–144.
20. Román, F.J.; Abad, F.J.; Escorial, S.; Burgaleta, M.; Martínez, K.; Álvarez-Linera, J.; Quiroga, M.Á.; Karama, S.; Haier, R.J.; Colom, R. Reversed hierarchy in the brain for general and specific cognitive abilities: A morphometric analysis. *Hum. Brain Map.* **2014**, *35*, 3805–3818. [CrossRef] [PubMed]
21. Steinmayr, R.; Spinath, B. Predicting school achievement from motivation and personality. *Z. Pädagogische Psychol.* **2007**, *21*, 207–216. [CrossRef]
22. Steinmayr, R.; Spinath, B. The importance of motivation as a predictor of school achievement. *Learn. Individ. Differ.* **2009**, *19*, 80–90. [CrossRef]
23. Steinmayr, R.; Ziegler, M.; Träuble, B. Do intelligence and sustained attention interact in predicting academic achievement? *Learn. Individ. Differ.* **2010**, *20*, 14–18. [CrossRef]
24. Zhang, J.; Ziegler, M. Interaction effects between openness and fluid intelligence predicting scholastic performance. *J. Intell.* **2015**, *3*, 91–110. [CrossRef]
25. Brogden, H.E.; Taylor, E.K. The theory and classification of criterion bias. *Educ. Psychol. Meas.* **1950**, *10*, 159–183. [CrossRef]
26. Spearman, C. *The Abilities of Man*; Macmillan: London, UK, 1927.
27. Deary, I.J.; Pagliari, C. The strength of g at different levels of ability: Have detterman and daniel rediscovered spearman's "law of diminishing returns"? *Intelligence* **1991**, *15*, 247–250. [CrossRef]
28. Kovacs, K.; Conway, A.R.A. Process overlap theory: A unified account of the general factor of intelligence. *Psychol. Inq.* **2016**, *27*, 151–177. [CrossRef]
29. Ackerman, P.L. Process overlap and g do not adequately account for a general factor of intelligence. *Psychol. Inq.* **2016**, *27*, 178–180. [CrossRef]
30. Stankov, L. Overemphasized "g". *J. Intell.* **2017**, *5*, 33. [CrossRef]
31. Schneider, W.J.; Newman, D.A. Intelligence is multidimensional: Theoretical review and implications of specific cognitive abilities. *Hum. Resour. Manag. Rev.* **2015**, *25*, 12–27. [CrossRef]
32. Ackerman, P.L.; Beier, M.E.; Boyle, M.O. Working memory and intelligence: The same or different constructs? *Psychol. Bull.* **2005**, *131*, 30–60. [CrossRef] [PubMed]
33. MacCann, C.; Joseph, D.L.; Newman, D.A.; Roberts, R.D. Emotional intelligence is a second-stratum factor of intelligence: Evidence from hierarchical and bifactor models. *Emotion* **2014**, *14*, 358–374. [CrossRef] [PubMed]
34. Reeve, C.L.; Meyer, R.D.; Bonaccio, S. Intelligence-personality associations reconsidered: The importance of distinguishing between general and narrow dimensions of intelligence. *Intelligence* **2006**, *34*, 387–402. [CrossRef]
35. Brunner, M.; Süß, H.M. Analyzing the reliability of multidimensional measures: An example from intelligence research. *Educ. Psychol. Meas.* **2005**, *65*, 227–240. [CrossRef]
36. Gignac, G.E.; Kretzschmar, A. Evaluating dimensional distinctness with correlated-factor models: Limitations and suggestions. *Intelligence* **2017**, *62*, 138–147. [CrossRef]
37. Ziegler, M.; Dietl, E.; Danay, E.; Vogel, M.; Bühner, M. Predicting training success with general mental ability, specific ability tests, and (un) structured interviews: A meta analysis with unique samples. *Int. J. Select. Assess.* **2011**, *19*, 170–182. [CrossRef]
38. Ziegler, M.; Brunner, M. Test standards and psychometric modeling. In *Psychosocial Skills and School Systems in the 21st Century*; Lipnevich, A.A., Preckel, F., Roberts, R., Eds.; Springer: Göttingen, Germany, 2016; pp. 29–55.
39. Wittmann, W.W. Multivariate reliability theory: Principles of symmetry and successful validation strategies. In *Handbook of Multivariate Experimental Psychology. Perspectives on Individual Differences*; Nesselroade, J.R., Cattell, R.B., Eds.; Plenum Press: New York, NY, USA, 1988; Volume 2, p. 966.
40. Coyle, T.R.; Snyder, A.C.; Richmond, M.C.; Little, M. Sat non-g residuals predict course specific gpas: Support for investment theory. *Intelligence* **2015**, *51*, 57–66. [CrossRef]

41. Lang, J.W.; Kersting, M.; Hülsheger, U.R.; Lang, J. General mental ability, narrower cognitive abilities, and job performance: The perspective of the nested-factors model of cognitive abilities. *Pers. Psychol.* **2010**, *63*, 595–640. [CrossRef]

42. Spinath, B.; Eckert, C.; Steinmayr, R. Gender differences in school success: What are the roles of students' intelligence, personality and motivation? *Educ. Res.* **2014**, *56*, 230–243. [CrossRef]

43. Carpenter, P.A.; Just, M.A.; Shell, P. What one intelligence test measures: A theoretical account of the processing in the raven progressive matrices test. *Psychol. Rev.* **1990**, *97*, 404–431. [CrossRef] [PubMed]

44. Deary, I.J.; Strand, S.; Smith, P.; Fernandes, C. Intelligence and educational achievement. *Intelligence* **2007**, *35*, 13–21. [CrossRef]

45. Greiff, S.; Heene, M. Why psychological assessment needs to start worrying about model fit. *Eur. J. Psychol. Assess.* **2017**, *33*, 313–317. [CrossRef]

46. Heene, M.; Hilbert, S.; Draxler, C.; Ziegler, M.; Bühner, M. Masking misfit in confirmatory factor analysis by increasing unique variances: A cautionary note on the usefulness of cutoff values of fit indices. *Psychol. Methods* **2011**, *16*, 319–336. [CrossRef] [PubMed]

47. Ziegler, M.; Danay, E.; Heene, M.; Asendorpf, J.; Bühner, M. Openness, fluid intelligence, and crystallized intelligence: Toward an integrative model. *J. Res. Personal.* **2012**, *46*, 173–183. [CrossRef]

48. Tucker-Drob, E.M. Differentiation of cognitive abilities across the life span. *Dev. Psychol.* **2009**, *45*, 1097–1118. [CrossRef] [PubMed]

49. Molenaar, D.; Dolan, C.V.; Wicherts, J.M.; van der Maas, H.L.J. Modeling differentiation of cognitive abilities within the higher-order factor model using moderated factor analysis. *Intelligence* **2010**, *38*, 611–624. [CrossRef]

50. Detterman, D.K.; Daniel, M.H. Correlations of mental tests with each other and with cognitive variables are highest for low IQ groups. *Intelligence* **1989**, *13*, 349–359. [CrossRef]

51. Deary, I.J.; Egan, V.; Gibson, G.J.; Austin, E.J.; Brand, C.R.; Kellaghan, T. Intelligence and the differentiation hypothesis. *Intelligence* **1996**, *23*, 105–132. [CrossRef]

52. Blum, D.; Holling, H. Spearman's law of diminishing returns. A meta-analysis. *Intelligence* **2017**, *65*, 60–66. [CrossRef]

53. Cortina, J.M. Interaction, nonlinearity, and multicollinearity: Implications for multiple regression. *J. Manag.* **1993**, *19*, 915–922. [CrossRef]

54. Yerkes, R.M.; Dodson, J.D. The relation of strength of stimulus to rapidity of habit-formation. *J. Comp. Neurol. Psychol.* **1908**, *18*, 459–482. [CrossRef]

55. Antonakis, J.; House, R.J.; Simonton, D.K. Can super smart leaders suffer from too much of a good thing? The curvilinear effect of intelligence on perceived leadership behavior. *J. Appl. Psychol.* **2017**, *102*, 1003–1021. [CrossRef] [PubMed]

56. Wonderlic. *Wonderlic Personnel & Scholastic Level Exam: User's Manual*; Wonderlic Personnel Test, Inc.: Libertyville, IL, USA, 2002.

57. Ganzach, Y.; Gotlibobski, C.; Greenberg, D.; Pazy, A. General mental ability and pay: Nonlinear effects. *Intelligence* **2013**, *41*, 631–637. [CrossRef]

58. Tett, R.P.; Burnett, D.D. A personality trait-based interactionist model of job performance. *J. Appl. Psychol.* **2003**, *88*, 500–517. [CrossRef] [PubMed]

59. Ziegler, M.; Bensch, D.; Maaß, U.; Schult, V.; Vogel, M.; Bühner, M. Big five facets as predictor of job training performance: The role of specific job demands. *Learn. Individ. Differ.* **2014**, *29*, 1–7. [CrossRef]

60. Gardner, R.G.; Harris, T.B.; Li, N.; Kirkman, B.L.; Mathieu, J.E. Understanding "it depends" in organizational research. *Organ. Res. Methods* **2017**, *20*, 610–638. [CrossRef]

61. McClelland, G.H.; Judd, C.M. Statistical difficulties of detecting interactions and moderator effects. *Psychol. Bull.* **1993**, *114*, 376–390. [CrossRef] [PubMed]

62. Siemsen, E.; Roth, A.; Oliveira, P. Common method bias in regression models with linear, quadratic, and interaction effects. *Organ. Res. Methods* **2009**, *13*, 456–476. [CrossRef]

63. Lantz, B. *Machine Learning with R*; Packt Publishing Ltd.: Birmingham, UK, 2015.

64. Simonsohn, U. Two-Lines: A Valid Alternative to the Invalid Testing of u-Shaped Relationships with Quadratic Regressions. Available online: https://ssrn.com/abstract=3021690 or http://dx.doi.org/10.2139/ssrn.3021690 (accessed on 21 March 2018).

65. Cortes, C.; Vapnik, V. Support-vector networks. *Mach. Learn.* **1995**, *20*, 273–297. [CrossRef]

66. Bleidorn, W.; Hopwood, C.J. Using machine learning to advance personality assessment and theory. *Personal. Soc. Psychol. Rev.* **2018**. [CrossRef] [PubMed]
67. Yarkoni, T.; Westfall, J. Choosing prediction over explanation in psychology: Lessons from machine learning. *Perspect. Psychol. Sci.* **2017**, *12*, 1–23. [CrossRef] [PubMed]
68. Sauer, S.; Buettner, R.; Heidenreich, T.; Lemke, J.; Berg, C.; Kurz, C. Mindful machine learning. *Eur. J. Psychol. Assess.* **2018**, *34*, 6–13. [CrossRef]
69. Kersting, M.; Althoff, K.; Jäger, A.O. *Wilde-Intelligenz-Test 2: Wit-2 [Wilde-Intelligence-Test 2: Wit 2]*; Hogrefe, Verlag für Psychologie: Göttingen, Germany, 2008.
70. Cumming, G. The new statistics: Why and how. *Psychol. Sci.* **2014**, *25*, 7–29. [CrossRef] [PubMed]
71. R Core Team. *R: A Language and Environment for Statistical Computing*; R Foundation for Statistical Computing: Vienna, Austria, 2014.
72. RStudio. *Rstudio: Integrated Development Environment for R (Version 1.1.419)*; Rstudio: Boston, MA, USA, 2012.
73. Revelle, W. *Psych: Procedures for Psychological, Psychometric, and Personality Research*; R Foundation for Statistical Computing: Vienna, Austria, 2016.
74. Behrendt, S. *Lm.Beta: Add Standardized Regression Coefficients to Lm-Objects. R Package Version 1.5-1*; R Foundation for Statistical Computing: Vienna, Austria, 2014. Available online: http://CRAN.R-project.org/package=lm.beta (accessed on 18 July 2018).
75. Xie, Y.H. *Knitr: A General-Purpose Package for Dynamic Report Generation in R. R Package Version 1.17*; R Foundation for Statistical Computing: Vienna, Austria, 2017.
76. Stanley, D. *Apatables: Create American Psychological Association (APA) Style Tables. R Package Version 1.5.1*; R Foundation for Statistical Computing: Vienna, Austria, 2017. Available online: https://CRAN.R-project.org/package=apaTables (accessed on 18 July 2018).
77. Kuhn, M. *Caret: Classification and Regression Training. R Package Version 6.0-77*; R Foundation for Statistical Computing: Vienna, Austria, 2017.
78. Wickham, H. *Tidyverse: Easily Install and Load'Tidyverse'Packages. R Package Version*; R Foundation for Statistical Computing: Vienna, Austria, 2017; Volume 1.
79. Wickham, H.; Hester, J.; Francois, R. *Readr: Read Rectangular Text Data. R Package Version 1.1.1*; R Foundation for Statistical Computing: Vienna, Austria, 2017.
80. Dalal, D.K.; Zickar, M.J. Some common myths about centering predictor variables in moderated multiple regression and polynomial regression. *Organ. Res. Methods* **2011**, *15*, 339–362. [CrossRef]
81. Gignac, G.E.; Szodorai, E.T. Effect size guidelines for individual differences researchers. *Personal. Individ. Differ.* **2016**, *102*, 74–78. [CrossRef]
82. Bosco, F.A.; Aguinis, H.; Singh, K.; Field, J.G.; Pierce, C.A. Correlational effect size benchmarks. *J. Appl. Psychol.* **2015**, *100*, 431–449. [CrossRef] [PubMed]
83. Lindqvist, E.; Vestman, R. The labor market returns to cognitive and noncognitive ability: Evidence from the Swedish enlistment. *Am. Econ. J. Appl. Econ.* **2011**, *3*, 101–128. [CrossRef]
84. Schipolowski, S.; Wilhelm, O.; Schroeders, U. On the nature of crystallized intelligence: The relationship between verbal ability and factual knowledge. *Intelligence* **2014**, *46*, 156–168. [CrossRef]
85. Ziegler, M.; Danay, E.; Schölmerich, F.; Bühner, M. Predicting academic success with the big 5 rated from different points of view: Self-rated, other rated and faked. *Eur. J. Personal.* **2010**, *24*, 341–355. [CrossRef]
86. Park, G.; Schwartz, H.A.; Eichstaedt, J.C.; Kern, M.L.; Kosinski, M.; Stillwell, D.J.; Ungar, L.H.; Seligman, M.E.P. Automatic personality assessment through social media language. *J. Personal. Soc. Psychol.* **2014**, *108*, 934–952. [CrossRef] [PubMed]
87. Chen, L.; Gong, T.; Kosinski, M.; Stillwell, D.; Davidson, R.L. Building a profile of subjective well-being for social media users. *PLoS ONE* **2017**, *12*, e0187278. [CrossRef] [PubMed]
88. Wang, Y.; Kosinski, M. Deep neural networks are more accurate than humans at detecting sexual orientation from facial images. *J. Personal. Soc. Psychol.* **2018**, *114*, 246–257. [CrossRef] [PubMed]

Journal of
Intelligence

MDPI

Article

Aligning Predictor-Criterion Bandwidths: Specific Abilities as Predictors of Specific Performance

Serena Wee [1,2]

1   School of Psychological Science, University of Western Australia, 35 Stirling Highway,
    Crawley, WA 6009, Australia; serena.wee@uwa.edu.au
2   School of Social Sciences, Singapore Management University, 90 Stamford Road, Level 4,
    Singapore 178903, Singapore

Received: 13 March 2018; Accepted: 25 June 2018; Published: 7 September 2018

Abstract: The purpose of the current study is to compare the extent to which general and specific abilities predict academic performances that are also varied in breadth (i.e., general performance and specific performance). The general and specific constructs were assumed to vary only in breadth, not order, and two data analytic approaches (i.e., structural equation modeling [SEM] and relative weights analysis) consistent with this theoretical assumption were compared. Conclusions regarding the relative importance of general and specific abilities differed based on data analytic approaches. The SEM approach identified general ability as the strongest and only significant predictor of general academic performance, with neither general nor specific abilities predicting any of the specific subject grade residuals. The relative weights analysis identified verbal reasoning as contributing more than general ability, or other specific abilities, to the explained variance in general academic performance. Verbal reasoning also contributed to most of the explained variance in each of the specific subject grades. These results do not provide support for the utility of predictor-criterion alignment, but they do provide evidence that both general and specific abilities can serve as useful predictors of performance.

Keywords: specific ability; second stratum abilities; academic performance; nested-factor models; relative importance analysis; predictor-criterion bandwidth alignment

1. Introduction

Measures of cognitive ability consistently correlate positively with other measures of cognitive ability. Spearman [1] initially argued that these positive correlations among tests (i.e., positive manifold), could be explained by a single, general ability factor, which he termed "*g*". In contrast, Thurstone [2] emphasized specific abilities in his work, postulating seven specific ability factors. Although the emerging consensus view synthesizes both these extreme positions into a single theoretical framework including both general and specific ability factors [3,4], the debate continues as to the theoretical relations between general and specific abilities [5–9]. The crux of the matter, to paraphrase Humphreys [5] (p. 91), is whether breadth only (as represented by the nested-factors model), or super-ordination also (as represented by the higher-order factor model), defines the general ability factor in relation to the specific ability factors.

As an extension of Spearman's original unidimensional model of cognitive ability, higher-order factor models assume that the higher-order factor (i.e., general ability) explains the positive correlations among lower-order factors (i.e., specific abilities) [7]. That is, both breadth and superordinate position define the theoretical relations between general and specific abilities. General ability is conceptualized more broadly than specific abilities, and because of its causal status, it is also of a higher order. In contrast, nested-factor models, also referred to as bi-factor models, assume that only breadth distinguishes between general and specific abilities [6,10–12]. (When only a few measures of cognitive ability are available, the non-*g* residuals may also be used to reflect specific abilities, in addition to measurement error [13,14].) Although general ability is conceptualized more broadly than specific abilities, it is not assumed to have a causal effect on specific abilities (i.e., they have the same order or position in a hierarchical arrangement) [5,7].

Most of the extant research has been based, implicitly or explicitly, on the assumption that the structure of cognitive abilities is best described by a higher-order factor model. That is, the relationship between a higher-order, general ability factor and a cognitive test variable is fully mediated by the lower-order specific ability factor. To elaborate, empirical tests (e.g., incremental validity analysis using multiple regression) that assign to the general ability factor all the variance that is common among the cognitive ability predictors and the dependent variable, can be argued to be consistent with such a theoretical assumption [8]. For example, in a hierarchical regression analysis, the multiple regression is conducted in steps. At each step, the proportion of variance explained by the predictors (i.e., R^2) is obtained. Typically, general ability is included in the first step. The R^2 attributed to general ability in this first step thus includes any of the variance that it shares with the specific abilities (i.e., common variance among cognitive ability predictors is attributed to general ability). Then in the second step, one or more specific abilities are included, and the incremental change in R^2 between steps is attributed to the specific abilities (i.e., only unique variance is attributed to specific abilities).

Research based on such tests could be interpreted as providing robust evidence for the utility of general ability as a predictor, and at best, only equivocal evidence for the utility of specific abilities as predictors. That is, although general ability (i.e., "*g*") has been consistently shown to be a useful predictor of practical outcomes such as academic and occupational performance [15–17], the utility of specific abilities as predictors of these same outcomes remains hotly contested. Specifically, researchers concluding that there is "not much more than *g*" have highlighted the modest ($\Delta R^2 \approx 0.02$) increments to validity afforded by specific abilities, most especially when a wide range of jobs are being considered [17–19]. At the extreme of this position, some have even argued that the continued investigation of specific abilities as predictors is unwarranted, e.g., [20] (p. 341). That said, it should be noted that even small increments in validity can translate into reasonably large practical gains (i.e., dollar utility) [21]. Nonetheless, other researchers have reached seemingly opposite conclusions. For example, when researchers focused on matching specific abilities to the criteria—i.e., perceptual and psychomotor abilities for a job requiring quick and accurate processing of simple stimuli—they found support for the incremental (i.e., unique) validity of specific abilities over *g* [22]. As noted earlier, the nested-factors model provides an alternative conceptualization of the structure of cognitive abilities. In this model, observed test variance is explained by two distinct ability factors: general ability and specific abilities. The general ability factor—distinguished from specific abilities by its breadth—explains variance in a greater number of observed variables than a specific ability factor. However, in this model, general ability is not assumed to cause specific abilities. That is, general ability is not a higher-order factor. Instead, general and specific abilities are all first-order factors. It should be noted that a nested-factors conceptualization of cognitive ability allows for correlations among the general and specific ability factors. However, in practice, when using structural equation modeling (SEM), it is common to assume independence among all the ability factors so as to reduce model complexity and enhance factor interpretability, e.g., [6,7,23]. When independent ability factors are assumed in the nested-factors model, it can be shown to be mathematically equivalent to a higher-order factor model (with additional proportionality constraints) [7].

Research based on a nested-factors model of cognitive ability, has more consistently found support for the utility of specific abilities as predictors, e.g., [6,8,13,14,24–26]. In a large sample of middle-school English students, verbal reasoning residuals (obtained by regressing the verbal ability measure on to the general ability measure) significantly predicted standardized exam scores in French [13], and similarly, numerical reasoning residuals significantly predicted national curriculum test scores in math [25]. In a study based on Swedish students, a numeric ability factor was found to correlate strongly with subject grades on a specific science factor [6]. Further, in a meta-analysis based on employed samples, verbal ability was found to account for more of the explained variance in overall job performance (in low-complexity jobs; as compared with a general ability measure) [8]. Similarly, in a sample of military personnel undergoing job-required training in a foreign language, foreign language aptitude was found to account for more of the explained variance (than general ability) in both training course grades, and in a performance-based oral proficiency interview [26].

Thus, previous research based on a nested-factors model of cognitive ability provides support for the utility of specific abilities as predictors of both academic and occupational outcomes. However, these studies differ from each other in at least two important ways: (a) in the alignment of the predictor and criterion bandwidth, and (b) in the data analytic approach used to examine the research question. First, whereas some studies examined the usefulness of specific abilities for predicting specific performance criteria (e.g., [6]), other studies examined their usefulness for predicting general criteria (e.g., [8]). Because some researchers [9,24,27–29] have alluded to how a lack of support for specific abilities could have been due to a misalignment between the bandwidth of the predictor and criterion measures, it is important to systematically examine how the alignment of predictor-criterion bandwidths could influence conclusions about the usefulness of cognitive ability predictors. To briefly elaborate on one such example, Wittman and Süß [29] drew on Brunswik's [30] lens model to develop the concept of Brunswik symmetry, which postulates that "every level of generality at the predictor model has its symmetrical level of generality at the criterion side" [29] (p. 79). And, based on this fundamental assumption, Wittman and Süß [29] therefore predicted that criterion validity is maximized to the extent that the predictor and the criterion are symmetric in their generality (i.e., aligned in the bandwidth of their respective constructs).

Second, these studies also differed in the specific data analytic approach used. Some data analytic approaches have focused on only the unique contribution of predictors as a way of determining the relative importance of general and specific abilities. In contrast, other data analytic approaches, collectively termed as relative importance analyses, have attempted to estimate a predictor's proportionate contribution to explained variance in the criteria—i.e., to reflect both a predictor's unique effect and its joint effect when considered with other predictors. As an example of the first type of data analytic approach, studies that have implemented a nested-factors model conceptualization of cognitive abilities using SEM have thus far assumed independence among the ability factors, e.g., [24]. The assumption of independence means that results from these studies will be similar to results obtained when ability is conceptualized using a higher-order factor model, given that these two models are mathematically related (as discussed earlier). That is, the conclusions drawn from both the hierarchical regression analysis (where general ability is entered in the first step of the model, and specific abilities is entered in the second step) or the SEM analysis (where ability factors are constrained to be independent) are likely to indicate the same relative importance ordering of general versus specific ability factors. However, one advantage of the SEM approach over the regression approach, is the ability to control for measurement error.

In the discussion of the SEM approach, the relative importance of a predictor over other predictors in a set is determined by the extent to which that predictor explains unique variance in the criterion. This method for partitioning variance works well if independent predictors are used. If predictors are correlated, as is—at least empirically—the case with cognitive ability predictors, then this approach does not adequately reflect either the direct effect that a specific ability predictor has on the criterion (its correlation with the criterion), nor its joint effect when considered with general ability (because only the unique effect of the predictor on the criterion is considered; common variance among predictors is attributed to general ability). Stated differently, to determine a predictor's relative importance, one needs to determine its contribution to the common variance in the criterion that has been accounted for by the set of predictors.

This is the problem addressed in the multiple regression literature on relative importance analysis (the second data analytic approach), where several alternative metrics have been developed to supplement the understanding that might be obtained from multiple regression (for a review see [31]):

e.g., general dominance weights [32], relative weights [33], and Pratt's [34] index, with each measure using a slightly different method to measure the relative importance of predictors. *General dominance weights* are obtained by calculating a predictor's incremental validity for each possible regression submodel in which it could be included, across all the possible submodels. For example, with $k = 4$ predictors, there are $2^4 - 1 = 15$ possible submodels, and a given predictor is included in eight of these submodels. The general dominance weight reflects a predictor's relative importance by indexing its overall average incremental validity across submodels, therefore capturing both its contribution to a criterion on its own and jointly with other predictors in the set. *Relative weights* use a different method to partition variance across predictors. Specifically, the k correlated predictors are transformed into a new set of k variables that are uncorrelated with each other, yet as highly correlated with the original predictors as possible. The criterion can be regressed onto this new set of variables to obtain one set of standardized regression coefficients, and the original variables can be regressed on to this new set of variables to obtain a second set of standardized regression coefficients. Multiplying these two sets of coefficients together therefore provides a measure of the relative contribution of a predictor (on its own and jointly with other predictors) to the variance explained in the criterion. *Pratt's index*, as an attempt to capture both unique and joint variance explained, is calculated as the product of a predictor's correlation (i.e., its contribution to explaining criterion variance on its own) and its standardized regression coefficient (i.e., its contribution to explaining criterion variance jointly with other predictors).

In this study, I utilized the relative weights [33] metric. This is because Pratt's index is not always interpretable (e.g., a negative product moment), and also because it has been shown that rank ordering of predictors in terms of their relative importance tend to be almost identical based on either the general dominance weights or the relative weights. However, relative weights have the added benefit of being computationally easier to obtain [35]. As has been previously highlighted, e.g., [6,8], different data analytic approaches can result in vastly different interpretations, even when using the same data set. It is therefore important to compare data analytic approaches to determine if the same or different conclusions are reached regarding (a) whether specific abilities are useful as predictors, and (b) whether the same specific abilities are identified.

In summary, the purpose of this paper is to examine the utility of specific abilities—in comparison with general ability—for predicting outcomes that are either broadly or narrowly defined. Further, to determine whether differing conclusions on the usefulness of specific abilities as predictors could result from different data analytic approaches, e.g., [8,26], I also compared results obtained from SEM to results obtained from relative weights analysis.

2. Materials and Methods

Please see the introductory article for a description of the sample and measures.

Analytic Strategy

Two data analytic approaches were used to examine the focal research question regarding the relative importance of general versus specific abilities in predicting general versus specific academic performance. In the SEM approach, all models were estimated based on individual-level data and analyzed using Mplus version 7.4 [36] with maximum-likelihood estimation. To evaluate model fit, I considered the incremental fit index provided by the comparative fit index (CFI; [37]), which compares the observed covariance matrix to a baseline model with uncorrelated latent variables, and the absolute fit indices provided by the root mean square error of approximation (RMSEA; [38]) and the standardized root mean square residual (SRMR; [39]). Following the recommendations provided by Hu and Bentler [39], the following cutoff values were used as indicators of good (or acceptable) model fit: CFI > 0.95 (>0.90), RMSEA < 0.06 (<0.08), and SRMR < 0.08.

For these analyses, an initial model was estimated that included only the relationship between a general ability factor and a general academic performance factor. The general ability factor was estimated by all the three cognitive ability tests and the general academic performance factor was estimated by all the four subject grades (χ^2 = 24.30, *df* = 13, *p* = 0.03, CFI = 0.958, RMSEA = 0.063, SRMR = 0.043). Examination of the modification indices indicated that allowing residuals of the language subjects (i.e., German and English) to be correlated would significantly improve fit, and the initial model was revised accordingly (see Figure 1; χ^2 = 9.01, *df* = 12, *p* = 0.70, CFI = 1.000, RMSEA = 0.000, SRMR = 0.027). For subsequent models, the residual variance for each indicator (see Figure 1: u1–u7) was used as a measure of the specific ability or specific criterion. Specifically, the unfolding residual variance was used as a measure of spatial reasoning, the analogies residual as a measure of verbal reasoning, the number series residual as a measure of numerical reasoning, and each of the specific subject grade residuals as a measure of specific performance in that subject.

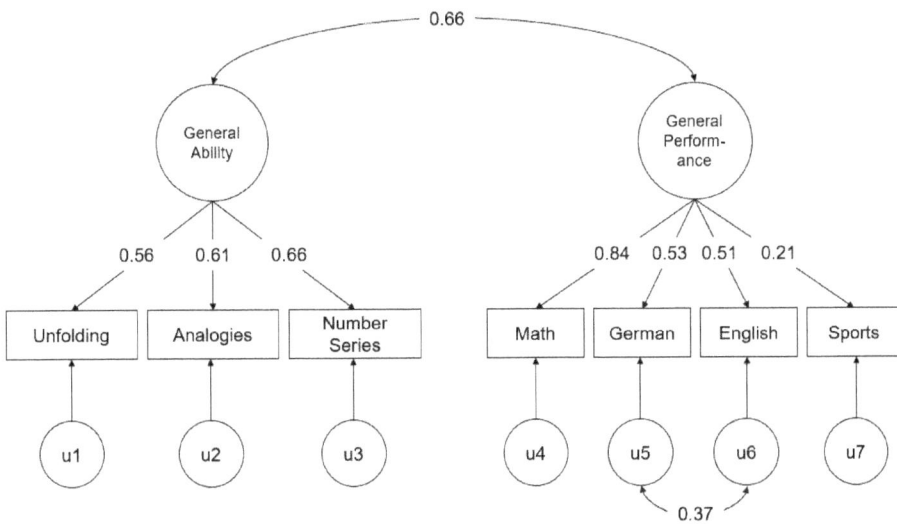

Figure 1. Fully standardized parameter estimates of the structural equation modeling (SEM) model between general ability and general academic performance. All parameter estimates significant at *p* < 0.01.

To test the incremental criterion-related validity of general ability for specific academic performance, I examined the validity of general ability for predicting each of the specific subject grade residuals (i.e., u4–u7 in Figure 1), controlling for the relationship between general ability and general academic performance. To test the incremental criterion-related validity of specific abilities for general academic performance, I examined the validity of each specific ability measure (i.e., u1–u3 in Figure 1), controlling for the relationship between general ability and general academic performance. And lastly, to test the incremental criterion-related validity of specific abilities for specific academic performance, I examined the validity of each specific ability measure, for each specific subject grade residual, controlling for the relationship between general ability and general academic performance. In total, 19 separate analyses were conducted, where the focal ability-performance path coefficient was examined.

In the second data analytic approach, relative weights analyses using ability factor scores were conducted. These factor scores were extracted from the item-level data. For example, the spatial reasoning ability factor score was obtained by fitting a unidimensional factor to the 20 items of the unfolding test, and the general ability factor score was obtained by fitting a unidimensional factor to all the 60 items from the unfolding, analogies, and number series tests. Ability factor scores were used in place of composite scores so as to obtain a general ability measure that was not perfectly collinear with the set of specific ability measures. General academic performance was calculated based on the simple average of all the four subject grades. A separate analysis was conducted for each of the five criteria: general academic performance, and each of the four specific academic performances (as measured by subject grades). The relative weights analyses were conducted based on the individual-level data, in the R statistical software (v. 3.4.1) [40] using the yhat package provided by Nimon, Oswald, and Roberts [41] (see also [42]).

3. Results

Table 1 presents the means, standard deviations, and correlations among the cognitive ability and subject grade variables. Correlations among the ability factors were all positive ($M = 0.56$; range: 0.32 to 0.86), with the highest correlations being between general ability and the specific abilities. Correlations among the specific subject grades were also all positive ($M = 0.46$; range: 0.11 to 0.79), with the highest correlations being between general academic performance and the specific subject grades. As expected, cognitive ability scores were positively related to subject grades ($M = 0.23$; range: -0.01 to 0.42), with the exception of the relationship between spatial reasoning (i.e., unfolding) and sports grades ($r = -0.01$, $p > 0.05$).

Table 1. Descriptive statistics for the overall sample ($N = 219$).

Variable	1.	2.	3.	4.	5.	6.	7.	8.	9.
1. General Performance	–								
2. Math	0.787	–							
3. German	0.775	0.439	–						
4. English	0.757	0.427	0.542	–					
5. Sports	0.442	0.183	0.156	0.108	–				
6. General Ability	0.372	0.424	0.261	0.251	0.029	–			
7. Unfolding	0.252	0.310	0.213	0.132	−0.014	0.732	–		
8. Analogies	0.348	0.348	0.236	0.272	0.066	0.652	0.321	–	
9. Number Series	0.300	0.349	0.185	0.212	0.033	0.865	0.397	0.392	–
M	4.127	3.808	3.913	3.735	5.050	0.000	0.000	0.000	0.000
SD	0.666	1.153	0.937	0.940	0.718	0.950	0.913	0.887	0.933

Note: Correlations $\geq |0.14|$ are statistically significant at $p < 0.05$.

Results from the SEM analysis are presented in Table 2. Controlling for the relationship between general ability and general academic performance ($r = 0.66$, $p < 0.01$; see Figure 1), the standardized path coefficients between the specific ability residuals and (general or specific) academic performance were estimated. After controlling for the relationship between general ability and general academic performance, none of the specific ability residuals significantly predicted general academic performance: unfolding = -0.06, analogies = 0.12, and number series = -0.09 (all ps > 0.05). General ability also did not significantly predict specific academic performance (i.e., subject grade residuals): math = 0.19, German = 0.00, English = 0.02, and sports = -0.016 (all ps > 0.05). And lastly, none of the specific ability-specific academic performance relationships were significant, after controlling for the relationship between general ability and general performance ($M = 0.00$; range: -0.10 to 0.08). Thus, these results do not provide support for the utility of specific ability predictors, after the taking into account the relationship between general ability and general academic performance.

Table 2. Standardized relationship between cognitive abilities and academic performance.

Variable	General Performance	Math (res)	German (res)	English (res)	Sports (res)
General Ability	–	0.19	0.00	0.02	−0.16
		(0.24)	(0.13)	(0.12)	(0.15)
Unfolding	−0.06	0.02	0.07	−0.09	−0.10
	(0.12)	(0.08)	(0.06)	(0.07)	(0.07)
Analogies	0.12	−0.02	−0.01	0.08	0.01
	(0.12)	(0.10)	(0.07)	(0.06)	(0.08)
Number Series	−0.09	0.04	−0.05	0.02	−0.09
	(0.19)	(0.10)	(0.07)	(0.07)	(0.08)

Note: Analyses were conducted separately for each of the 19 standardized path coefficients, controlling for the relationship between general ability and general academic performance. res = residual, i.e., the residual variance after removing variance due to general ability or general academic performance. Standard errors are reported in parentheses.

Table 3 presents the results for the relative weights analysis (i.e., raw and scaled weights) for general academic performance and for each specific academic grade. For ease of comparison with traditional regression-based metrics, it also presents the correlation, and standardized and unstandardized regression coefficients. Besides the correlation coefficient, all other metrics were obtained from regression models that included all four ability predictors.[1] Overall, the variance accounted for by ability predictors was 18.4% in general academic performance, 21.9% in math grades, 8.4% in German grades, 10.0% in English grades, and 1.1% in sports grades. Of the four ability predictors, general ability showed the strongest correlation with general academic performance ($r = 0.37$). Based on the bootstrapped 95% CI of the difference between pairs of values, this correlation is significantly stronger than the correlations between general academic performance with either unfolding ($r = 0.25$), or number series ($r = 0.30$), but not with analogies ($r = 0.35$). When ability predictors are considered jointly (i.e., regression coefficients) unfolding ($b = 0.81$), analogies ($b = 0.73$), and number series ($b = 1.16$) provide unique, positive contributions to variance explained in general academic performance. Also, general ability is now negatively related to general academic performance ($b = -1.74$), making these regression results somewhat difficult to interpret. In contrast, the relative weights capture both a predictor's unique and shared contribution to explaining variance in the criterion. General ability contributed to 3.7% of the explained variance in general academic performance, and hence contributed to 20.1% (=0.037/0.184) of the total explained variance in general academic performance. Similarly, unfolding, analogies, and number series contributed to 15.7%, 40.8%, and 23.4% of the total explained variance in general academic performance, respectively. Thus, relative weights indicated that, when a predictor's shared and unique contribution to the explained variance in the criterion were considered simultaneously, verbal reasoning (i.e., analogies) was found to be a more important predictor of general academic performance than was general ability (i.e., 40.8% vs. 20.1%). However, the bootstrapped 95% CI of the difference between the raw weights indicate that this difference is not statistically significant.

---

[1] These results are supplemented by a hierarchical regression analysis showing the incremental contribution (over general ability) of each specific ability by itself, in a pair, and in a triplet (see Appendix A Table A1).

Table 3. Regression-based metrics of predictor variable importance.

Metric	General Ability	Unfolding	Analogies	Number Series
General Performance ($R^2 = 0.184$)				
r	0.372 (0.232, 0.497) [a, b]	0.252 (0.121, 0.382) [a]	0.348 (0.223, 0.472)	0.300 (0.155, 0.431) [b]
b	−1.745 (−3.303, 0.014) [a, b, c]	0.814 (0.113, 1.450) [a]	0.732 (0.171, 1.258) [b]	1.163 (0.090, 2.083) [c]
B	−2.489 (−4.658, 0.018) [a, b, c]	1.115 (0.166, 1.964) [a]	0.976 (0.235, 1.684) [b]	1.628 (0.131, 2.869) [c]
Raw weight	0.037 (0.020, 0.068)	0.029 (0.006, 0.070)	0.075 (0.025, 0.151)	0.043 (0.012, 0.094)
Scaled weight	20.109%	15.761%	40.761%	23.370%
Math Performance ($R^2 = 0.219$)				
r	0.424 (0.302, 0.545) [a, b]	0.310 (0.175, 0.436) [a]	0.348 (0.222, 0.472)	0.349 (0.216, 0.480) [b]
b	−3.133 (−5.604, −0.360) [a, b, c]	1.521 (0.380, 2.512) [a, d]	1.262 (0.344, 2.063) [a, e]	2.130 (0.453, 3.656) [c, d, e]
B	−2.580 (−4.690, −0.295) [a, b, c]	1.204 (0.311, 2.036) [a, d]	0.971 (0.269, 1.587) [a, e]	1.722 (0.360, 2.942) [c, d, e]
Raw weight	0.047 (0.028, 0.082)	0.046 (0.014, 0.099)	0.067 (0.022, 0.141)	0.058 (0.021, 0.119)
Scaled weight	21.560%	21.101%	30.734%	26.606%
German Performance ($R^2 = 0.084$)				
r	0.261 (0.132, 0.382) [a]	0.213 (0.077, 0.350)	0.236 (0.101, 0.350)	0.185 (0.052, 0.319) [a]
b	−1.021 (−3.478, 1.376)	0.566 (−0.478, 1.621)	0.496 (−0.277, 1.287)	0.681 (−0.780, 2.094)
B	−1.035 (−3.396, 1.478)	0.551 (−0.487, 1.566)	0.469 (−0.253, 1.222)	0.678 (−0.760, 2.074)
Raw weight	0.017 (0.008, 0.042)	0.022 (0.003, 0.074)	0.032 (0.005, 0.081)	0.013 (0.002, 0.047)
Scaled weight	20.238%	26.190%	38.095%	15.476%
English Performance ($R^2 = 0.100$)				
r	0.251 (0.114, 0.387) [a]	0.132 (0.001, 0.273) [a]	0.272 (0.135, 0.391)	0.212 (0.074, 0.360)
b	−1.907 (−4.060, 0.475)	0.817 (−0.160, 1.755)	0.828 (0.081, 1.565)	1.268 (−0.093, 2.554)
B	−1.927 (−4.169, 0.470)	0.793 (−0.153, 1.708)	0.781 (0.069, 1.464)	1.258 (−0.089, 2.546)
Raw weight	0.019 (0.008, 0.045)	0.006 (0.001, 0.038)	0.051 (0.010, 0.115)	0.024 (0.004, 0.069)
Scaled weight	19.000%	6.000%	51.000%	24.000%
Sports Performance ($R^2 = 0.011$)				
r	0.029 (−0.102, 0.159)	−0.014 (−0.145, 0.116)	0.066 (−0.072, 0.198)	0.033 (−0.105, 0.164)
b	−0.921 (−2.675, 0.882)	0.352 (−0.401, 1.110)	0.345 (−0.206, 0.912)	0.571 (−0.496, 1.648)
B	−1.217 (−3.620, 1.131)	0.447 (−0.521, 1.476)	0.426 (−0.259, 1.106)	0.742 (−0.657, 2.180)
Raw weight	0.002 (0.001, 0.020)	0.000 (0.000, 0.020)	0.006 (0.000, 0.041)	0.003 (0.000, 0.029)
Scaled weight	18.182%	0.000%	54.545%	27.273%

Note: r = correlation coefficient, b = standardized regression coefficient, B = unstandardized regression coefficient, Raw weight = raw relative weight, Scaled weight = rescaled relative weight (sums to 100 within row). Bootstrapped 95% CI are presented in parentheses. Subscripts (i.e., a–e) indicate statistically significant differences in pairs of metrics (within rows).

Based on the relative weights, verbal reasoning (i.e., analogies) was also the most important predictor for math (30.7%), German (38.1%), English (51.0%), and sports (54.5%) grades. That is, it contributed to a greater proportion of total explained variance than did general ability in each subject grade: math (21.6%), German (20.2%), English (19.0%), and sports (18.2%). Although these results may be consistent with expectations for German and English grades—i.e., in addition to contributing to the shared variance explained, verbal reasoning also contributed uniquely to performance in language-based subjects—the obtained results are somewhat surprising for math and sports grades. For both these subjects, although verbal reasoning was found to be the most important predictor, numerical reasoning (i.e., number series) was ranked second in importance: math (26.6%) and sports (27.3%). However, as with the results for general academic performance, bootstrapped 95% CIs indicated that none of the differences between raw weights are statistically significant. Lastly, general ability accounted for about 20% of the explained variance in the various performance criteria, which means that, taken together, the specific abilities accounted for about 80% of total explained variance in the performance criteria. These results suggest that specific abilities (especially verbal reasoning) are useful predictors of both general and specific academic performance.

4. Discussion

In order to advance the discussion on the usefulness of general and specific abilities for predicting performance, this study examined the validity of these abilities when predicting broadly versus narrowly defined criteria. The SEM approach identified general ability as the strongest (and only) predictor of general academic performance; it explained 44% of the variance in general academic performance. In contrast, the relative weights analysis identified verbal reasoning (i.e., analogies) as a more important predictor of general academic performance than even general ability. Specifically, of the 18% of the variance jointly accounted for by the ability predictors, general ability's proportionate contribution was 20% while verbal reasoning's proportionate contribution was double this at 41%. These results are consistent with much of the previous literature. As reviewed in the introduction, the SEM approach consistently identifies general ability as an important predictor of broadly defined criteria, e.g., [24], whereas several studies based on the relative weights approach have identified verbal ability/verbal reasoning as the most important predictor of broadly defined criteria such as overall job performance (at least in low complexity jobs) [8] and training grades [26].

Further, the SEM approach indicated that neither general nor specific abilities significantly predicted specific academic performance (i.e., subject grade residuals), once the relationship between general ability and general academic performance was accounted for. In contrast, relative weights analysis identified verbal reasoning as the most important predictor for each of the specific subject grades. In sum, at least based on these data, these results do not provide evidence for the utility of aligning predictor and criterion bandwidth for maximizing validity. Instead, these results suggest that, although general and specific abilities can serve as useful predictors of performance, conclusions regarding their utility depended critically on the data analytic approach used.

There are several plausible explanations for the differences in the pattern of results across approaches. Although both data analytic approaches were based on a nested-factors conceptualization of the cognitive abilities, the ability constructs were still operationalized differently across approaches. In the SEM approach, the general and specific abilities were constrained to not share any variance, whereas in the relative weights analysis, cognitive abilities were allowed to correlate with one another. Thus, to the extent that general and specific abilities are actually correlated, the SEM model is therefore mis-specified and the accuracy of our conclusions regarding the utility of general versus specific abilities reduced. For example, one possible way that general and specific abilities could be correlated is if multiple, discrete cognitive processes interact dynamically, resulting in an emergent, observed positive manifold across cognitive tests (i.e., general ability). Based on this theoretical mechanism, the correlation between general ability and a specific ability (e.g., verbal reasoning) occurs to the degree that the specific ability results from the interactions over time of a subset of the cognitive processes that are also involved in the emergence of the general factor. The relative weights analysis does not require independent predictors, and therefore is able to more accurately capture the proportionate contribution of individual predictors to explaining variance in the criteria. However, even though relative weights analysis was developed specifically to determine the relative importance of correlated predictors, the method is still based on multiple regression. Therefore, it does not remove the underlying issue of multicollinearity (when it exists). In this dataset, for example, general ability was quite highly correlated ($rs > 0.70$) with the specific abilities. As a consequence, confidence intervals around the point estimates are also fairly wide. Thus, although verbal reasoning was identified as contributing more than general ability to explained variance across all criteria, the difference in these raw relative weights (for each criterion) was not statistically significant at $p < 0.05$.

Perhaps just as importantly, the data analytic approaches also differed in how the performance constructs were operationalized. Whereas the SEM analyses used specific performance measures that excluded general performance variance, the relative weights analyses used specific performance measures that included both general and specific performance variance. Further, it should be noted that a unidimensional model of performance (with correlated language grade residuals) fit the data extremely well ($\chi^2_{(12)} = 9.01$, $p = 0.70$). This suggests that academic performance is adequately described by just a single performance factor; the specific subject grade residuals might not have served as adequate or reliable indicators of specific subject grade performance, once variance associated with general academic performance was removed.

Taken together, these results show that data analytic approaches can have implications as to which specific abilities are identified as useful predictors of specific performance criteria. Thus, this research suggests that even when data analytic approaches are based on the same theoretical assumptions (in this case, based on the nested-factor model of cognitive abilities) it is still possible that substantively different conclusions regarding specific abilities can be reached. Consequently, future research efforts should be directed toward better understanding how data analytic approaches can impact our conclusions regarding the usefulness of a given specific ability predictor.

Limitations and Future Research Directions

A number of study limitations should be noted. First, and perhaps most critically, only a small number of measures were available for the cognitive ability predictors, and for the performance criteria. Even if it could be reasonably argued that the general ability and general performance constructs were adequately captured by these measures, this argument is unlikely to extend to the construct-valid assessment of either the specific ability or specific performance constructs. That is, in this study, across both data analytic approaches, measures of the specific constructs included both specific construct variance, as well as error variance. Stated differently, unreliable measures diminish our ability to derive useful and interpretable specific factors [43,44]. In turn, because general and specific ability predictors differ in how reliably they are measured, this obfuscates our ability to meaningfully evaluate their usefulness as predictors.

Second, it should be noted that a substantial portion of the variance in general and specific academic performance was unexplained by cognitive ability. This is most notable, for example, with the specific performance criterion of sports grades, where general and specific abilities together explained only 1.1% of the variance in the criterion. This suggests that non-cognitive individual difference constructs (such as interests, personality, or motivation) or group difference variables (such as sex or race) also have a role to play in predicting academic performance. Specifically, theoretical arguments regarding the interplay of interests and motivations in determining domain-relevant specific abilities (i.e., knowledge and skills), e.g., [45,46], as well as empirical research demonstrating how interests and abilities are mutually causal over time [47], suggest that a fruitful avenue for better understanding the usefulness of specific abilities for predicting consequential outcomes resides in disentangling the dynamic relationships between specific abilities and specific interests, as they jointly predict performance over time.

This paper examined the utility of aligning the bandwidth of predictors to criteria. Although no support was found for the utility of alignment, this might have been because the previously identified limitations did not allow this proposition to be adequately tested. Further, this study also highlights the value of explicitly considering the criterion when evaluating the usefulness of cognitive ability predictors. Because there are important practical criteria (beyond performance) that relate to cognitive abilities, an evaluation of the predictive utility of cognitive abilities should also consider these other criteria (e.g., sex, race and adverse impact potential) in addition to, or in conjunction with, performance. For example, research by Wee, Newman, and Joseph [48] demonstrated that the use of specific abilities, rather than general ability, could improve an organization's diversity outcomes, even whilst maintaining expected job performance at levels that would be obtained from a general ability predictor.

Lastly, in this paper, positive manifold was taken as evidence that there is a general ability factor, i.e., a common cause that provides a parsimonious account for a substantial portion of the variance in cognitive ability measures. However, there are several plausible explanations for how observed variables could be positively correlated even in the absence of such an underlying, causal general factor [49–53]. Although a general ability construct provides an extremely effective and efficient predictor of performance across a wide variety of domains [15–17], it does not appear to have significantly advanced our understanding of the manner in which cognitive ability relates to important practical outcomes (i.e., "*g* is poorly defined and poorly understood" [54], p. 3). A set of less parsimonious—but more substantively interpretable—specific abilities could provide the alternative required to develop a better articulated theory of how cognitive ability relates to practical outcomes, and in so doing, further enhance the value of specific abilities as predictors of these same outcomes.

Conflicts of Interest: The author declares no conflict of interest.

Appendix A

Table A1. Hierarchical regression analysis.

Subset	R^2	Unfolding (U)	Analogies (A)	Number Series (N)
General Academic Performance				
General Ability (G)	0.138	0.001	0.019	0.002
G,U	0.139		0.019	0.008
G,A	0.157	0.000		0.001
G,N	0.140	0.007	0.018	
G,U,A	0.158			0.026
G,U,N	0.147		0.037	
G,A,N	0.158	0.026		
G,U,A,N	0.184			
Math Performance				
G	0.180	0.000	0.009	0.001
G,U	0.180		0.010	0.002
G,A	0.189	0.001		0.000
G,N	0.181	0.001	0.008	
G,U,A	0.190			0.029
G,U,N	0.182		0.037	
G,A,N	0.189	0.030		
G,U,A,N	0.219			
German Performance				
G	0.068	0.001	0.008	0.006
G,U	0.069		0.010	0.006
G,A	0.076	0.004		0.002
G,N	0.074	0.001	0.003	
G,U,A	0.079			0.005
G,U,N	0.075		0.009	
G,A,N	0.078	0.006		
G,U,A,N	0.084			
English Performance				
G	0.063	0.006	0.020	0.000
G,U	0.069		0.016	0.007
G,A	0.083	0.001		0.004
G,N	0.063	0.013	0.024	
G,U,A	0.084			0.016
G,U,N	0.076		0.024	
G,A,N	0.087	0.013		
G,U,A,N	0.100			
Sports Performance				
G	0.001	0.003	0.004	0.000
G,U	0.003		0.002	0.001
G,A	0.005	0.001		0.002
G,N	0.001	0.003	0.006	
G,U,A	0.006			0.005
G,U,N	0.004		0.007	
G,A,N	0.007	0.004		
G,U,A,N	0.011			

References

1. Spearman, C. "General intelligence", objectively determined and measured. *Am. J. Psychol.* **1904**, *15*, 201–292. [CrossRef]
2. Thurstone, L.L. Psychological implications of factor analysis. *Am. Psychol.* **1948**, *3*, 402–408. [CrossRef] [PubMed]
3. Carroll, J.B. *Human Cognitive Abilities: A Survey of Factor Analytic Studies*; Cambridge University Press: Cambridge, UK, 1993.
4. McGrew, K.S. CHC theory and the human cognitive abilities project: Standing on the shoulders of the giants of psychometric intelligence research. *Intelligence* **2009**, *37*, 1–10. [CrossRef]
5. Humphreys, L.G. The primary mental ability. In *Intelligence and Learning*; Friedman, M., Das, J., O'Connor, N., Eds.; Plenum Press: New York, NY, USA, 1981; pp. 87–102.
6. Gustafsson, J.-E.; Balke, G. General and specific abilities as predictors of school achievement. *Multivar. Behav. Res.* **1993**, *28*, 407–434. [CrossRef] [PubMed]
7. Yung, Y.-F.; Thissen, D.; Mcleod, L.D. On the relationship between the higher-order factor model and the hierarchical factor model. *Psychometrika* **1999**, *64*, 112–128. [CrossRef]
8. Lang, J.W.B.; Kersting, M.; Hülsheger, U.R.; Lang, J. General mental ability, narrower cognitive abilities, and job performance: The perspective of the nested-factors model of cognitive abilities. *Pers. Psychol.* **2010**, *63*, 595–640. [CrossRef]
9. Schneider, W.J.; Newman, D.A. Intelligence is multidimensional: Theoretical review and implications of specific cognitive abilities. *Hum. Resour. Manag. Rev.* **2015**, *25*, 12–27. [CrossRef]
10. Holzinger, K.J.; Swineford, F. The bi-factor method. *Psychometrika* **1937**, *2*, 41–54. [CrossRef]
11. Carroll, J.B. The higher-stratum structure of cognitive abilities: Current evidence supports g and about ten broad factors. In *The Scientific Study of General Intelligence: Tribute to Arthur R. Jensen*; Nyborg, H., Ed.; Elsevier Science/Pergamon Press: New York, NY, USA, 2003.
12. Reise, S.P. The rediscovery of bifactor measurement models. *Multivar. Behav. Res.* **2012**, *47*, 667–696. [CrossRef] [PubMed]
13. Deary, I.J.; Strand, S.; Smith, P.; Fernandes, C. Intelligence and educational achievement. *Intelligence* **2007**, *35*, 13–21. [CrossRef]
14. Coyle, T.R.; Purcell, J.M.; Snyder, A.C.; Kochunov, P. Non-g residuals of the SAT and ACT predict specific abilities. *Intelligence* **2013**, *41*, 114–120. [CrossRef]
15. Gottfredson, L.S. Why g matters: The complexity of everyday life. *Intelligence* **1997**, *24*, 79–132. [CrossRef]
16. Kuncel, N.R.; Hezlett, S.A.; Ones, D.S. Academic performance, career potential, creativity, and job performance: Can one construct predict them all? *J. Pers. Soc. Psychol.* **2004**, *86*, 148–161. [CrossRef] [PubMed]
17. Schmidt, F.L.; Hunter, J. General mental ability in the world of work: Occupational attainment and job performance? *J. Pers. Soc. Psychol.* **2004**, *86*, 162–173. [CrossRef] [PubMed]
18. Ree, M.J.; Earles, J.A. Predicting training success: Not much more than g. *Pers. Psychol.* **1991**, *44*, 321–332. [CrossRef]
19. Ree, M.J.; Earles, J.A.; Teachout, M.S. Predicting job performance: Not much more than g. *J. Appl. Psychol.* **1994**, *79*, 518–524. [CrossRef]
20. Hunter, J.E. Cognitive ability, cognitive aptitudes, job knowledge, and job performance. *J. Vocat. Behav.* **1986**, *29*, 340–362. [CrossRef]
21. Schmidt, F.L.; Hunter, J.E. The validity and utility of selection methods in personnel psychology: Practical and theoretical implications of 85 years of research findings. *Psychol. Bull.* **1998**, *124*, 262–274. [CrossRef]
22. Mount, M.K.; Oh, I.-S.; Burns, M. Incremental validity of perceptual speed and accuracy over general mental ability. *Pers. Psychol.* **2008**, *61*, 113–139. [CrossRef]
23. Mulaik, S.A.; Quartetti, D.A. First order of higher order general factor? *Struct. Equ. Model.* **1997**, *4*, 193–211. [CrossRef]
24. Reeve, C.L. Differential ability antecedents of general and specific dimensions of declarative knowledge: More than g. *Intelligence* **2004**, *32*, 621–652. [CrossRef]

25. Calvin, C.M.; Fernandes, C.; Smith, P.; Visscher, P.M.; Deary, I.J. Sex, intelligence and educational achievement in a national cohort of over 175,000 11-year-old schoolchildren in England. *Intelligence* **2010**, *38*, 424–432. [CrossRef]

26. Stanhope, D.S.; Surface, E.A. Examining the incremental validity and relative importance of specific cognitive abilities in a training context. *J. Pers. Psychol.* **2014**, *13*, 146–156. [CrossRef]

27. Visweswaran, C.; Ones, D.S. Agreements and disagreements on the role of general mental ability (GMA) in industrial, work, and organizational psychology. *Hum. Perform.* **2002**, *15*, 211–231.

28. Krumm, S.; Schmidt-Atzert, L.; Lipnevich, A.A. Specific cognitive abilities at work: A brief summary from two perspectives. *J. Pers. Psychol.* **2014**, *13*, 117–122. [CrossRef]

29. Wittmann, W.W.; Süß, H.-M. Investigating the paths between working memory, intelligence, knowledge, and complex problem-solving performances via Brunswik symmetry. In *Learning and Individual Differences: Process, Trait, and Content Determinants*; Ackerman, P.L., Kyllonen, P.C., Roberts, R.D., Eds.; American Psychological Association: Washington, DC, USA, 1999.

30. Brunswik, E. *Perception and the Representative Design of Psychological Experiments*; University of California Press: Berkeley, CA, USA, 1956.

31. Johnson, J.W.; LeBreton, J.M. History and use of relative importance indices in organizational research. *Org. Res. Methods* **2004**, *7*, 238–257. [CrossRef]

32. Budescu, D.V. Dominance analysis: A new approach to the problem of relative importance of predictors in multiple regression. *Psychol. Bull.* **1993**, *114*, 542–551. [CrossRef]

33. Johnson, J.W. A heuristic method for estimating the relative weight of predictor variables in multiple regression. *Multivar. Behav. Res.* **2000**, *35*, 1–19. [CrossRef] [PubMed]

34. Pratt, J.W. Dividing the indivisible: Using simple symmetry to partition variance explained. In Proceedings of the 2nd Tampere Conference in Statistics, Tampere, Finland, 1–4 June 1987; Pukilla, T., Duntaneu, S., Eds.; University of Tampere: Tampere, Finland, 1987.

35. LeBreton, J.M.; Ployhart, R.E.; Ladd, R.T. A Monte Carlo comparison of relative importance methodologies. *Org. Res. Methods* **2004**, *7*, 258–282. [CrossRef]

36. Muthen, L.K.; Muthen, B.O. *MPlus User's Guide*, 7th ed.; Muthen & Muthen: Los Angeles, CA, USA, 2012.

37. Bentley, P.M. *EQS Structural Equations Program Manual*; Multivariate Software: Encino, CA, USA, 1995.

38. Browne, M.W.; Cudeck, R. Alternative ways of assessing model fit. *Sociol. Methods Res.* **1992**, *21*, 230–258. [CrossRef]

39. Hu, L.-T.; Bentler, P.M. Cutoff criteria for fit indexes in covariance structure analysis: Conventional criteria versus new alternatives. *Struct. Equ. Model.* **1999**, *6*, 1–55. [CrossRef]

40. R Core Team. *R: A Language and Environment for Statistical Computing*; R Foundation for Statistical Computing: Vienna, Austria, 2015.

41. Nimon, K.F.; Oswald, F.L.; Roberts, J.K. *yhat: Interpreting Regression Effects*; R Package Version 2.0-0; R Foundation for Statistical Computing: Vienna, Austria, 2015.

42. Nimon, K.F.; Oswald, F.L. Understanding the results of multiple linear regression: Beyond standardized regression coefficients. *Org. Res. Methods* **2013**, *16*, 650–674. [CrossRef]

43. Haberman, S.J. When can subscores have value? *J. Educ. Behav. Stat.* **2008**, *33*, 204–229. [CrossRef]

44. Haberman, S.J.; Sinharay, S. Reporting of subscores using multidimensional item respond theory. *Psychometrika* **2010**, *75*, 209–227. [CrossRef]

45. Ackerman, P.L. A theory of adult intellectual development: Process, personality, interests, and knowledge. *Intelligence* **1996**, *22*, 227–257. [CrossRef]

46. Eccles (Parsons), J.S.; Adler, T.F.; Futterman, R.; Goff, S.B.; Kaczala, C.M.; Meece, J.L.; Midgley, C. Expectations, values, and academic behaviors. In *Perspectives on Achievement and Achievement Motivation*; Spence, J., Ed.; Freeman: San Francisco, CA, USA, 1983.

47. Denissen, J.J.; Zarrett, N.R.; Eccles, J.S. I like to do it, I'm able, and I know I am: Longitudinal couplings between domain-specific achievement, self-concept, and interest. *Child Dev.* **2007**, *78*, 430–447. [CrossRef] [PubMed]

48. Wee, S.; Newman, D.A.; Joseph, D.L. More than *g*: Selection quality and adverse impact implications of considering second-stratum cognitive abilities. *J. Appl. Psychol.* **2014**, *99*, 547–563. [CrossRef] [PubMed]

49. Thomson, G.H. A hierarchy without a general factor. *Br. J. Psychol.* **1916**, *8*, 271–281.

50. Van Der Maas, H.L.J.; Dolan, C.V.; Grasman, R.P.P.P.; Wicherts, J.M.; Huizenga, H.M.; Raijmakers, M.E.J. A dynamical model of general intelligence: The positive manifold of intelligence by mutualism. *Psychol. Rev.* **2006**, *113*, 842–861. [CrossRef] [PubMed]
51. Kan, K.-J.; Kievit, R.A.; Dolan, C.; Van der Maas, H. On the interpretation of the CHC factor Gc. *Intelligence* **2011**, *39*, 292–302. [CrossRef]
52. Wee, S.; Newman, D.A.; Song, Q.C. More than *g*-factors: Second-stratum factors should not be ignored. *Ind. Organ. Psychol.* **2015**, *8*, 482–488. [CrossRef]
53. Campbell, J.P. All general factors are not alike. *Ind. Organ. Psychol.* **2015**, *8*, 428–434. [CrossRef]
54. Murphy, K.R. What can we learn from "not much more than *g*"? *J. Intell.* **2017**, *5*, 8. [CrossRef]

Journal of
Intelligence

MDPI

Commentary

Non-*g* Factors Predict Educational and Occupational Criteria: More than *g*

Thomas R. Coyle

Department of Psychology, University of Texas at San Antonio, One UTSA Circle, San Antonio, TX 78249, USA;
thomas.coyle@utsa.edu; Tel.: +1-210-458-7407; Fax: +1-210-458-5728

Received: 11 March 2018; Accepted: 8 June 2018; Published: 7 September 2018

Abstract: In a prior issue of the *Journal of Intelligence*, I argued that the most important scientific issue in intelligence research was to identify specific abilities with validity beyond *g* (i.e., variance common to mental tests) (Coyle, T.R. Predictive validity of non-*g* residuals of tests: More than *g*. *Journal of Intelligence* 2014, 2, 21–25.). In this Special Issue, I review my research on specific abilities related to non-*g* factors. The non-*g* factors include specific math and verbal abilities based on standardized tests (SAT, ACT, PSAT, Armed Services Vocational Aptitude Battery). I focus on two non-*g* factors: (a) *non-g residuals*, obtained after removing *g* from tests, and (b) *ability tilt*, defined as within-subject differences between math and verbal scores, yielding math tilt (math > verbal) and verbal tilt (verbal > math). In general, math residuals and tilt positively predict STEM criteria (college majors, jobs, GPAs) and negatively predict humanities criteria, whereas verbal residuals and tilt show the opposite pattern. The paper concludes with suggestions for future research, with a focus on theories of non-*g* factors (e.g., investment theories, Spearman's Law of Diminishing Returns, Cognitive Differentiation-Integration Effort Model) and a magnification model of non-*g* factors.

Keywords: general intelligence (*g*); non-*g* factors; specific abilities; ability tilt; non-*g* residuals

---

1. Introduction

This paper begins with the parable of the blind men and an elephant. In the original parable, a group of blind men touch different parts of an elephant and reach different conclusions. One man touches the tusk and believes the elephant is a spear; another touches a leg and believes it is a tree; yet another touches the trunk and believes it is a snake. A modified version of the parable can illustrate a key problem in intelligence research: distinguishing general intelligence (*g*) and specific abilities. In the modified version, the elephant represents *g* and its parts represent specific abilities such as math ability, verbal ability, and spatial ability. The blind men are intelligence researchers who focus on a specific ability, ignoring the overlap between the specific ability and *g*. These "blind" intelligence researchers may incorrectly conclude that the specific ability predicts a criterion when it derives its predictive power entirely from *g*.

A lesson of the modified parable is that the predictive power of a specific ability (beyond *g*) can only be assessed *after removing g*, which is related to all cognitive abilities. The current paper reviews research on the predictive power of specific abilities for diverse criteria (e.g., college grades, college majors, jobs) after removing *g*. The focus is on specific abilities (e.g., math and verbal) measured by standardized tests. The tests include the SAT (formerly, Scholastic Aptitude Test) and ACT (formerly, American College Test), two college admissions tests taken by high school students; the Preliminary SAT (PSAT), an eligibility test used by the National Merit Scholarship Program and taken by high school students; and the Armed Services Vocational Aptitude Battery (ASVAB), a selection test used by the US Armed Forces. The SAT, ACT, PSAT, and ASVAB are strongly related to IQ and *g* and are available in datasets with large and representative samples such as the National Longitudinal Survey of Youth (NLSY) (e.g., [1], p. 19; see also, [2,3]).

The focus on non-*g* factors is consistent with my view that the most important scientific issue in intelligence research is to identify non-*g* factors with validity beyond *g* (cf. [4], p. 21). As discussed below, my research on non-*g* factors calls into question the primacy of *g* hypothesis, which assumes that *g* explains the predictive power of cognitive tests and that non-*g* factors have negligible predictive power (cf. [5]). In contrast to this hypothesis, my research shows that non-*g* factors predict diverse criteria, that non-*g* effects are substantial in size (βs $\approx$ 0.30), and that non-*g* effects are consistent with theories of intelligence (e.g., investment theories).

The paper is divided into four sections. The first section discusses the predictive validity of *g* and non-*g* factors. The second section reviews a key study [6] that launched my research program on non-*g* factors. The next three sections discuss my subsequent research on non-*g* factors, ending with a review of studies by other researchers. The final section discusses directions for future research, highlighting theories of non-*g* factors and a magnification model of non-*g* factors.

2. *g* and Non-*g* Factors: The Primacy of *g*

A key distinction in intelligence research is between *g*, which represents variance common to cognitive tests, and non-*g* factors, which represent variance obtained after (statistically) removing *g* from tests. *g* can be identified in a factor analysis of diverse cognitive tests, which typically shows that the first factor (dubbed *g*) explains more variance among tests than any other factor (e.g., [7], pp. 73–88). The basis of *g* is *positive manifold*. Positive manifold refers to positive correlations among diverse cognitive tests, which indicate that people who do well on one test tend to do well on all others.

g is one of the best predictors of school and work performance (for a review, see [7], pp. 270–305; see also, [8,9]). Moreover, a test's *g* loading (i.e., its correlation with *g*) is directly related to its predictive power. In general, tests with strong *g* loadings correlate strongly with school and work criteria, whereas tests with weak *g* loadings correlate weakly with such criteria. For example, Jensen ([7], p. 280) found that the *g* loadings of the Wechsler Adult Intelligence Scale (WAIS) subtests were directly related to their predictive power for school criteria (e.g., school grades and class ranks). WAIS subtests with stronger *g* loadings generally predicted school criteria well, whereas subtests with weaker *g* loadings predicted such criteria poorly. Consistent with these findings, Thorndike [10] found that *g* explained most of the predictable variance in academic achievement (80–90%), whereas non-*g* factors (obtained after removing *g* from tests) explained a much smaller portion of variance (10–20%). Similar results have been found for job training and productivity, which are robustly related to *g* but negligibly related to non-*g* factors of tests (e.g., $r_{\text{non-}g}$ < 0.10, [7], pp. 283–285; see also, [9,11]).

The totality of evidence supports the primacy of *g* hypothesis, which assumes that *g* largely explains the predictive power of tests and that non-*g* factors have limited or negligible predictive power. Contrary to the primacy of *g* hypothesis, my research shows that non-*g* factors of standardized tests (e.g., SAT, ACT, PSAT) robustly predict educational and occupational criteria, with non-*g* effects often being substantial in size (βs $\approx$ 0.30).[1]

3. A Foundational Study by Coyle and Pillow [6]: Non-*g* Residuals Predict College GPA

Non-*g* factors are operationalized as factors obtained after statistically removing *g* from tests. In the current paper, the focus is on non-*g* factors of standardized tests drawn from the 1997 NLSY (*N* = 8989). The tests include the SAT, ACT, PSAT, and ASVAB. Special attention is given to the SAT and ACT, two college admissions tests that measure math and verbal abilities. The SAT and ACT correlate moderately with college GPA (*r* = 0.43) and strongly with IQ tests and a *g* based on the ASVAB (*r* = 0.78) ([6], p. 274; see also, [2,3]). The ASVAB is a selection test used by the US Armed

---

[1] Peterson and Brown ([12], p. 180) show that the relation between β and *r* is independent of sample size and number of predictors and that the imputation of *r* (given β) yields an estimate similar to the population statistic (ρ) (for a criticism of Peterson and Brown's [12] approach, see [13]). Given the robust relationship between β and *r*, βs of 0.10, 0.30, and 0.50 could be described as small, medium, and large, respectively, using Cohen's [14] criteria for correlations.

Forces. It includes 12 diverse cognitive tests, which measure two academic abilities (math and verbal) and two non-academic abilities (shop/technical skills and mental speed). In most studies (described below), non-*g* factors of the SAT, ACT, and PSAT are obtained after removing a *g* based on the ASVAB and are correlated with the specific abilities of the ASVAB and with other criteria (e.g., college majors and jobs).

A foundational study by Coyle and Pillow [6] examined the predictive power of non-*g* residuals of the SAT and ACT (obtained after removing *g*) for first-year college GPA. The study is foundational in the sense that it precipitated my later research, which examined other non-*g* factors and other criteria (e.g., specific GPAs, college majors, jobs). The study has an interesting history. The initial results were obtained using simple regressions and data from a university sample. The analysis regressed college GPA on SAT and ACT scores after removing *g* (*g* was based on the Wonderlic, a word recall test, and other tests). Surprisingly, the SAT and ACT predicted college GPA after removing *g*, which generally explains the predictive power of tests (e.g., [7], pp. 270–305).

The results were submitted to *Intelligence* and returned with suggestions for revisions. A key suggestion was to replicate the results with a more representative sample and a more sophisticated analytical approach. The NLSY was identified as a good data source because it contained a large and representative sample (N = 8989) as well as college GPAs, SAT and ACT scores, and ASVAB scores. Using the NLSY, structural equation modeling estimated *g* and non-*g* factors. *g* was estimated using the ASVAB, and the non-*g* residuals of the SAT and ACT (obtained after removing *g*) were correlated with college GPA (Figure 1). The key result was that the non-*g* residuals of the SAT and ACT predicted college GPA almost as well as *g* predicted college GPA (βs ≈ 0.30).[2] The results are inconsistent with the primacy of *g* hypothesis, which assumes that non-*g* factors have negligible predictive power (cf. [5]).

What might explain the predictive power of SAT and ACT non-*g* residuals (for college GPA)? One possibility is that the SAT and ACT measure specific abilities with predictive power for college GPA, which reflects an amalgam of traits. Such traits include math and verbal abilities, which are a staple of college curricula and may predict college GPA. This possibility led to subsequent research (discussed below), which focused on the predictive power of non-*g* residuals of the SAT and ACT math and verbal subtests.

---

[2]   The main analyses analyzed SAT and ACT composite scores, which were the sum of the math and verbal subtest scores. The results replicated in separate analyses of SAT and ACT subtest scores.

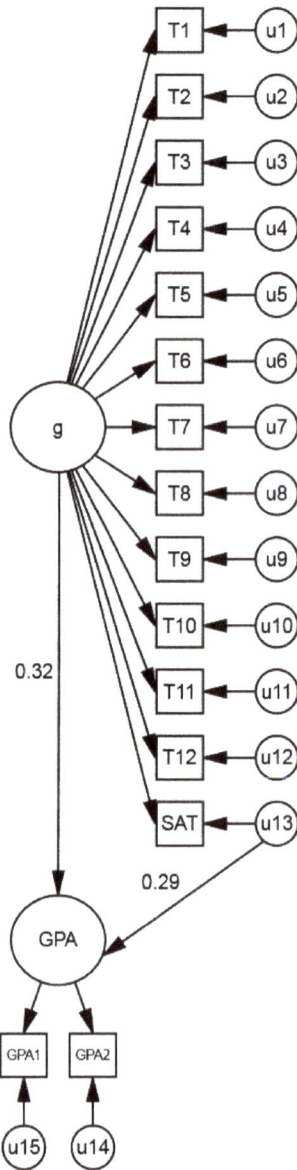

Figure 1. Model of *g* with the SAT, ASVAB tests (T1–T12), and college GPA. A parallel model (not shown) analyzed the ACT. The symbol "u13" represents the non-*g* residuals of SAT composite scores (math + verbal), obtained after removing *g*. The u13→GPA path estimates the relation of the SAT non-*g* residuals with GPA (β = 0.29). Figure adapted from Coyle and Pillow [6].

4. Non-*g* Residuals of the SAT and ACT Predict Specific Abilities and GPAs

The study by Coyle and Pillow [6] fueled additional research on non-*g* residuals. In a subsequent study, Coyle, Purcell, Snyder, and Kochunov [15] examined the predictive power of non-*g* residuals of the SAT and ACT math and verbal subtests (obtained after removing *g*) for specific abilities on the

ASVAB. The ASVAB consisted of 12 tests: arithmetic reasoning (AR), assembling objects (AO), auto information (AI), coding speed (CS), electronics information (EI), general science (GS), math knowledge (MK), mechanical comprehension (MC), numerical operations (NO), paragraph comprehension (PC), shop information (SI), and word knowledge (WK). These tests estimated four abilities (indicators): verbal ability (GS, PC, WK), math ability (AR, AO, MK), shop ability (AI, EI, SI, MC), and mental speed (CS, NO). The four abilities were correlated with the non-*g* residuals of the SAT and ACT math and verbal subtests (Figure 2).

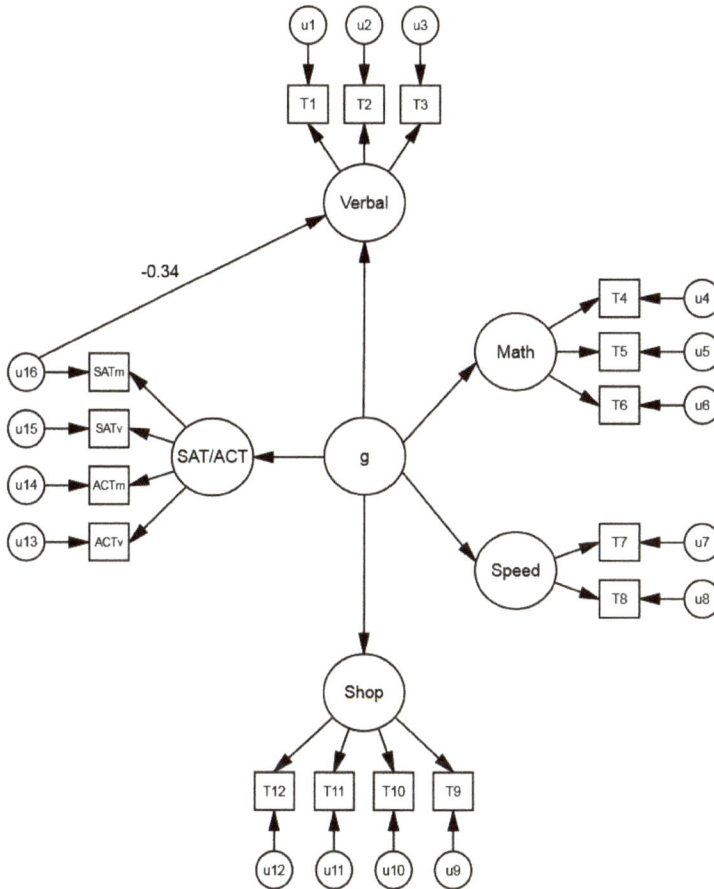

Figure 2. Model of *g* with the SAT subtests, ACT subtests, ASVAB abilities. The symbol "u16" represents the SAT math non-*g* residuals (based on the math subtest), obtained after removing *g*. The u16→Verbal path estimates the relation of the SAT math non-*g* residuals with ASVAB verbal ability (β = −0.34). Figure adapted from Coyle et al. [15].

Coyle et al. [15] found a domain-specific pattern of effects between the non-*g* residuals of the SAT and ACT subtests and the math and verbal abilities of the ASVAB. The math residuals of the SAT and ACT correlated positively with math ability (M_β = 0.29) and negatively with verbal ability (M_β = −0.32). In contrast, the verbal residuals of the SAT and ACT correlated positively with verbal ability (M_β = 0.29) and negatively with math ability (M_β = −0.25) (The non-*g* residuals of the SAT and ACT correlated negligibly with the ASVAB shop and speed abilities, demonstrating discriminant validity).

Coyle et al. [15] interpreted the results in terms of investment theories ([16], pp. 138–146), which assume that investment in a specific ability (e.g., math) boosts similar abilities but retards competing abilities (e.g., verbal). Math residuals presumably reflect investment in math, which boosts math ability. In contrast, verbal residuals presumably reflect investment in verbal areas, which boosts verbal ability. In addition, because time is limited, investment in one ability (math) comes at the expense of investment in competing abilities (verbal), yielding negative relations between competing abilities (e.g., math and verbal).

Would Coyle et al.'s [15] results be replicated with college grades, which the SAT and ACT were designed to predict? This question was addressed by Coyle, Snyder, Richmond, and Little [17], who examined relations of SAT math and verbal non-g residuals with subject specific GPAs, using the College Board Validity Study dataset (N = 160,670). SAT scores were obtained for the math, reading, and writing subtests. College GPAs were obtained for courses in two categories: science, technology, engineering, and math (STEM), which were math loaded, and humanities, which were verbally loaded. g was based on an SAT factor, estimated using SAT scores; a STEM factor, estimated using STEM GPAs (e.g., math, science, engineering); and a humanities factor, estimated using humanities GPAs (e.g., English, history, foreign languages) (Figure 3). The non-g residuals of each SAT subtest (obtained after removing g) were correlated with the STEM and humanities factors.

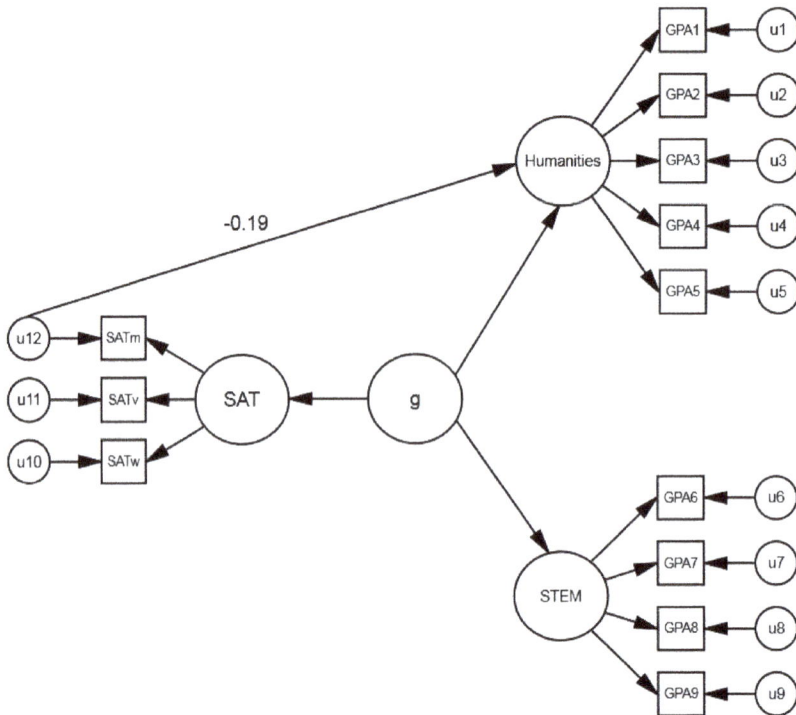

Figure 3. Model of g with STEM and humanities GPA factors. g was based on an SAT factor, estimated using SAT scores; a STEM factor, estimated using STEM GPAs, and a humanities factor, estimated using humanities GPAs. The non-g residuals of the SAT subtests, obtained after removing g, were correlated with the STEM and humanities factors. The model shows the relation of the SAT math non-g residuals with the humanities factor (β = −0.19). Figure adapted from Coyle, Snyder, Richmond, and Little [17].

Coyle, Snyder, Richmond, and Little's [17] results confirmed the domain-specific pattern obtained with the ASVAB abilities. SAT math residuals correlated positively with the math-based STEM GPA factor and negatively with the verbal-based humanities GPA factor. Conversely, SAT verbal residuals (reading and writing) showed the opposite pattern. The mean absolute effect ($|M_\beta| \approx 0.17$) was smaller than the mean absolute effect for the ASVAB abilities ($|M_\beta| \approx 0.29$) (cf. [15]). (The smaller effect could be attributed to the use of GPAs, which are less reliable than standardized test scores.) The results confirm the predictive power of non-*g* residuals and are inconsistent with the primacy of *g* hypothesis, which assumes that non-*g* factors have negligible predictive power. In addition, the results are consistent with investment theories. SAT math residuals presumably reflect investment in math, which boosts STEM GPAs but retards humanities GPAs. In contrast, SAT verbal residuals presumably reflect investment in verbal areas, which yields the opposite pattern of effects.

5. Ability Tilt Predicts Diverse Criteria

Another non-*g* factor with predictive power is ability tilt, defined as the within-subject difference in math and verbal scores on standardized tests such as the SAT and ACT. The within-subject difference yields two types of tilt: *math tilt*, which occurs when math scores are higher than verbal scores, and *verbal tilt*, which occurs when verbal scores are higher than math scores. Both types of tilt are unrelated to *g* but, like the SAT and ACT non-*g* residuals, still predict STEM and humanities criteria.

Lubinski, Benbow, and colleagues (for a review see, [18]; see also, [19–22]) were the first to define and systematically examine ability tilt in the Study of Mathematically Precocious Youth (SMPY). The SMPY is a longitudinal study of intellectually gifted youth (top 1% or higher) who took the SAT around age 12 years and were tracked into adulthood. The SMPY estimated *ability level* using SAT sum scores (math plus verbal), which correlate strongly with *g*, and *ability tilt* using SAT difference scores (math minus verbal), which are unrelated to *g*. Whereas ability level correlated positively with adult achievements (e.g., income and education), ability tilt (math or verbal) predicted the domain of achievement. Math tilt predicted STEM achievements (STEM degrees, patents, engineering jobs), whereas verbal tilt predicted humanities achievements (e.g., humanities degrees, books published, journalism jobs) [18].

Would the results of the SMPY replicate with a representative sample? The question is important because the SMPY involves gifted subjects (top 1% in ability). Moreover, ability tilt is a type of ability specialization (math or verbal), which may vary with ability level. In particular, differentiation theories assume that cognitive abilities become more differentiated (and less *g* loaded) at higher ability levels, which are associated with more ability specialization (e.g., [23]). An implication is that ability specialization should be more pronounced for SMPY subjects than for a representative sample of (lower ability) subjects, who should show less ability specialization and less tilt, which is a type of ability specialization.

Coyle, Purcell, Snyder, and Richmond ([24]; see also, [25]) examined ability tilt using a representative sample with a wider range of ability. The sample was drawn from the NLSY, a representative sample of youth in the United States. (The NLSY was also used in the studies of non-*g* residuals.) As in the studies of non-*g* residuals (e.g., [15]), the ASVAB estimated two academic abilities (math, verbal) and two non-academic abilities (speed, shop). Ability tilt (math tilt and verbal tilt) was based on math and verbal scores from the SAT and ACT, which are typically taken in grades 11 or 12, and from the PSAT, which is typically taken in grade 10. Tilt scores on the SAT, ACT, and PSAT were correlated with the four ASVAB abilities (after removing *g*) and also with college majors and jobs in STEM (e.g., engineering) and humanities (e.g., English).

Coyle et al.'s ([24]; see also, [25]) results confirmed the results of the SMPY (cf. [18]). Math tilt on all three tests (SAT, ACT, PSAT) correlated positively with ASVAB math ability and negatively with ASVAB verbal ability, whereas verbal tilt showed the opposite pattern ($|M_\beta| \approx 0.28$). (Math and verbal tilt correlated negligibly with the non-academic shop and speed abilities, demonstrating divergent validity.) In addition, math tilt predicted STEM majors and jobs, whereas verbal tilt predicted humanities majors and jobs ($|M_\beta| \approx 0.35$). The results confirm the predictive power of non-g factors and are inconsistent with the primacy of g hypothesis, which assumes that non-g factors have negligible predictive validity. In addition, the results are consistent with investment theories ([16], pp. 138–146). Ability tilt presumably reflects investment in math or verbal abilities, which boost similar abilities and preferences (e.g., math tilt and STEM) and inhibit competing abilities and preferences (e.g., math tilt and humanities).

Coyle et al.'s [24] results were extended in separate analyses of sex differences [25] and race differences (whites and blacks) [26]. The results indicated that mean levels of math tilt were higher for males (than females) and for whites (than blacks), whereas mean levels of verbal tilt were similar between groups. Similar to Coyle et al.'s [24] initial research (with undifferentiated groups), tilt was correlated with ASVAB abilities, college majors, and jobs, separately for each sex (males and females) and race (whites and blacks). The results replicated for all groups. Despite group differences in mean levels of tilt, math tilt generally predicted STEM criteria (STEM jobs, majors, abilities), whereas verbal tilt generally predicted humanities criteria (humanities jobs, majors, abilities). The results suggest that tilt relations (with diverse criteria) are not specific to a particular sex or race but apply to all groups.

A Non-g Nexus Involving Non-g Group Factor Residuals

Whereas the prior studies focused on non-g factors of a single test (e.g., SAT or ACT), a recent study by Coyle [27] focused on non-g residuals of group factors (based on multiple tests). The group factors were based on the ASVAB abilities (math, verbal, shop, speed) and were estimated using multiple tests with data from the NLSY (Figure 4). In general, group factors should yield more accurate estimates of non-g effects than individual tests (e.g., SAT and ACT), which are loaded with unique test-specific variance. As in the prior studies, the non-g residuals of the group factors were correlated with performance criteria (test scores and tilt scores on the SAT, ACT, and PSAT) and preference criteria (majors and jobs) in STEM and humanities.

Coyle's [27] results confirmed the predictive power of non-g residuals of the ASVAB group factors. Math residuals correlated positively with math/STEM criteria (test scores, tilt scores, college majors, jobs) and negatively with verbal/humanities criteria. In contrast, verbal residuals showed the opposite pattern. The mean effect size was medium to large ($|M_\beta| = 0.51$) [14]. (The shop and speed residuals generally correlated negligibly with all criteria, providing divergent validity.) The results were interpreted in terms of a non-g nexus involving non-g residuals of group factors and diverse criteria. The non-g nexus complements Jensen's ([7], pp. 544–583) notion of a "g nexus" involving g and diverse criteria. Like the tilt effects, the non-g nexus suggests trade-offs, with investment in a specific ability (reflected by non-g residuals) boosting similar abilities (e.g., math) but inhibiting competing abilities (e.g., verbal).

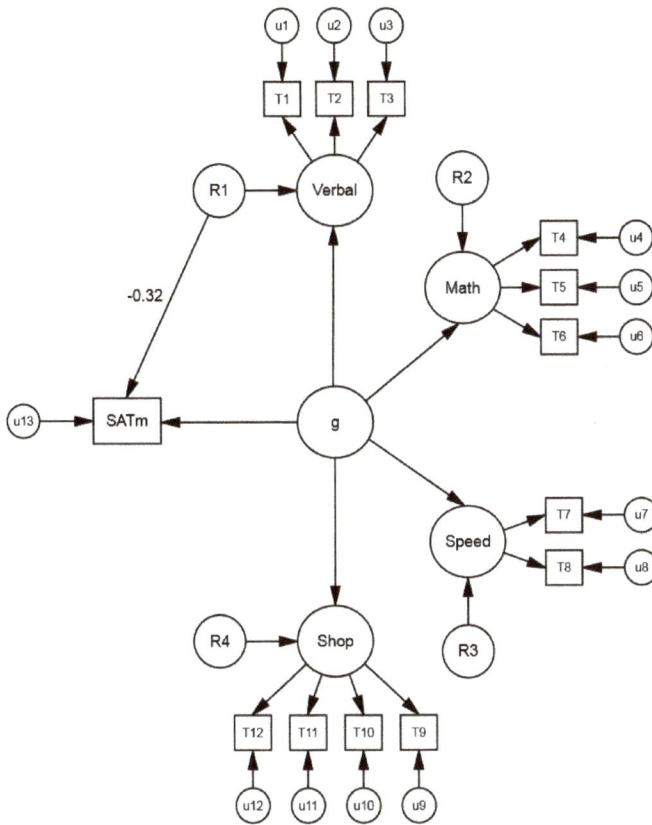

Figure 4. Model of *g* with ASVAB abilities (math, verbal, speed, shop). The symbol "R1" represents the ASVAB verbal non-*g* residuals, obtained after removing *g*. The R1→SAT math path estimates the relation of the ASVAB verbal non-*g* residuals with the SAT math subtest (β = −0.32). Figure adapted from Coyle [27].

6. Standing on the Shoulders of Giants: Other Research on Non-*g* Factors

Isaac Newton ([28], p. 416) said, "If I have seen further it is by standing on ye sholders of Giants". In this section, I would like to acknowledge some key studies that inspired my research on non-*g* factors and that bolster the predictive power of non-*g* factors. The studies examine non-*g* factors for countries other than the United States, cognitive abilities other than those sampled by the ASVAB, SAT, and ACT, and ability levels other than those sampled by the NLSY.

Calvin, Fernandez, Smith, Visscher, and Deary [29] examined non-*g* residuals linked to specific abilities (math and verbal) in 175,000 English students (in the UK) who received the Cognitive Abilities Test (CAT), which includes tests of verbal, quantitative, and non-verbal reasoning. Non-*g* residuals of each test were estimated (after removing *g*), and correlated with each other and with the raw scores of each test. Consistent with Coyle et al.'s [15] results, the math residuals correlated positively with the math (raw) scores and negatively with the verbal scores, whereas the verbal residuals showed the opposite pattern. The effect sizes ranged from moderate to strong ($|M_r| = 0.31$, range = −0.21 to 0.40) ([29], p. 427). Moreover, the effects were based on a large and representative sample of participants and tests, inspiring confidence in the results.

Johnson and Bouchard [30] analyzed data from the Minnesota Study of Twins Reared Apart (MISTRA) (*N* = 436) using the Verbal-Perceptual-Rotation (VPR) model. The VPR model involves a fourth-stratum *g*, three broad third-stratum factors (verbal, perceptual, rotation), and several narrow second-stratum factors linked to specific test performance (e.g., verbal, scholastic, number, speed, spatial, image rotation). The non-*g* residuals of the second-stratum factors (obtained after removing *g*) were correlated with each other ([30], p. 31). A key finding was the strong negative correlations of the verbal residuals with the spatial and rotational residuals ($M_r = -0.55$), which predict math/STEM criteria (e.g., [25,31]). The residual correlations of the VPR verbal and spatial abilities are analogous to the residual correlations of the ASVAB verbal and math abilities. Both sets of correlations are negative, which suggests a tradeoff between competing abilities (e.g., verbal-spatial or verbal-math). The tradeoff is consistent with investment theories, which predict that investment in one ability (e.g., verbal) comes at the expense of investment in competing abilities (e.g., spatial), yielding negative effects.

As discussed above, Lubinski, Benbow, and colleagues published seminal research on ability tilt using SAT scores from gifted students (top 1% in ability) in the SMPY (for a review, see [18]). SAT tilt scores (math minus verbal) were unrelated to SAT sum scores (math plus verbal), which correlate strongly with *g* (e.g., [2]). Despite being unrelated to *g*, tilt scores predicted diverse criteria in STEM and humanities. The criteria included favorite course in high school, college major, graduate degrees, technology patents, books published, and occupations. In general, math tilt predicted STEM criteria, whereas verbal tilt predicted humanities criteria. The results laid a foundation for my studies on tilt and non-*g* residuals using a representative sample from the NLSY (e.g., [27]).

Together, the studies reviewed in this section, along with my studies, confirm the predictive power of non-*g* factors (ability tilt and non-*g* residuals) for diverse criteria (e.g., GPAs, college majors, college degrees, jobs). Collectively, the studies yield a pattern of results that replicates with different samples (NLSY, SMPY, MISTRA), tests (SAT, ACT, PSAT, ASVAB, CAT), abilities (math, verbal, spatial), and models (VPR model, ASVAB model), supporting the robustness of non-*g* effects.

7. Future Directions: There is Nothing More Practical than a Good Theory

Kurt Lewin ([32], p. 169) said, "There is nothing more practical than a good theory". Good theories generate new hypotheses, facilitate interpretation of results, and guide future research. This last section reviews areas for future research, focusing on theories related to non-*g* factors. The theories include investment theories, Spearman's Law of Diminishing Returns (SLODR), and the Cognitive Differentiation-Integration Effort (CD-IE) model. The section also discusses alternative types of ability tilt (e.g., technical tilt) and alternative non-*g* factors (e.g., non-academic factors) and concludes with a magnification model of non-*g* factors.

As noted, investment theories are widely used to interpret non-*g* effects ([16], pp. 138–146; see also, [25–27]). Such theories assume that differential investment of time and effort influences specific abilities (unrelated to *g*) and preferences. Investment in STEM is assumed to boost math abilities, which leads to math tilt and STEM preferences. In contrast, investment in the humanities is assumed to boost verbal abilities, which leads to verbal tilt and humanities preferences. Future research should examine whether continued investment (over time) in a particular area influences non-*g* effects. One prediction is that continued investment would boost specific abilities and strengthen non-*g* effects. Such a pattern may be observed in university settings, with continued investment in a particular field of study (e.g., math/STEM or verbal/humanities) increasing the influence of non-*g* effects (e.g., ability tilt and non-*g* residuals).

Another relevant theory is Spearman's Law of Diminishing Returns (SLODR). SLODR is based on Spearman's ([33], p. 219) observation that correlations among mental tests generally decrease at higher ability levels, presumably because tests become less loaded with *g* (variance common to tests) and more loaded with non-*g* factors (variance unrelated to *g*). SLODR has received empirical support. In general, correlations and *g* loadings of tests decrease, and non-*g* effects increase, at higher ability levels [34]. The decrease in *g* (and increase in non-*g* effects) is assumed to reflect cognitive differentiation and specialization at higher ability levels, which boosts specialized abilities. The specialized abilities include verbal and math abilities (e.g., tilt and non-*g* residuals), which are unrelated to *g*. Future research should examine whether the effects of tilt and non-*g* residuals increase at higher ability levels, as predicted by SLODR.[3]

A third theory is based on the Cognitive Differentiation-Integration Effort (CD-IE) model [35,36]. CD-IE is an evolutionary model with implications for investment in mating effort versus ability specialization in specific areas (e.g., math or verbal). CD-IE distinguishes between fast and slow life histories, which are associated with different levels of mating effort versus educational specialization, which increases ability specialization (and non-*g* effects). Fast life histories are associated with high levels of mating effort and less educational investment, yielding less ability specialization and weaker non-*g* effects. In contrast, slow life histories are associated with low levels of mating effort and more educational investment, yielding more ability specialization and stronger non-*g* effects. The predictions of the CD-IE model have been confirmed using ASVAB scores from the NLSY (1979 cohort), which showed increased non-*g* variance (reflecting specialization) at slower life history levels [36]. Future research should examine whether life history influences ability tilt, non-*g* residuals, and other non-*g* factors. Based on CD-IE theory, non-*g* factors should become more pronounced at slower life history speeds, reflecting greater educational specialization and less investment in mating effort.

It should be noted that all three theories (investment theories, SLODR, CD-IE) predict that non-*g* effects increase nonlinearly with ability specialization (cf. [1,27]). In particular, non-*g* effects are expected to strengthen over time with factors that influence ability specialization (e.g., ability level, life history, education level), which magnify non-*g* effects. The predicted pattern is consistent with niche picking theories [37] and experience producing drive theories [38]. Both theories assume that non-*g* effects are magnified over time as people seek out and select activities compatible with their predispositions. The predispositions include preferences for specific activities (e.g., STEM or humanities), which accelerate the development of specific abilities and magnify non-*g* effects.

Another area for future research concerns alternative types of ability tilt. Tilt is typically based on the difference between math and verbal scores on standardized tests (e.g., SAT, ACT). The difference yields math tilt (math > verbal) and verbal tilt (verbal > math). Future research could explore two other types of tilt: *spatial tilt*, defined as the difference between spatial scores and other scores (e.g., math or verbal), and *technical tilt*, defined as the difference between shop/technical scores and other scores (e.g., math or verbal). Spatial tilt would reflect elevated spatial abilities, which predict STEM achievements [31]. Technical tilt would reflect elevated technical abilities (e.g., cars, electronics, tools), which may predict non-academic pursuits and jobs (e.g., mechanic, carpenter). Both types of tilt could be measured using tests of spatial and technical abilities (e.g., the ASVAB). In addition, both types of tilt could be used to examine predictions related to ability specialization. As with other types of tilt, high levels of spatial and technical tilt would be predicted at higher ability levels and at slower life histories, which accelerate ability specialization. In contrast, lower levels of spatial and technical tilt would be predicted at lower ability levels and at faster life histories, which inhibit specialization.

A final suggestion, related to the prior one (on tilt measures), concerns the abilities sampled in non-*g* studies, which focus on academic abilities (math and verbal). An open question is whether similar results would be found for non-academic abilities such as shop or technical abilities. Preliminary evidence on the question comes from Coyle's ([27], p. 22) analysis of non-*g* residuals for the non-academic shop factor (based on the ASVAB), which was correlated with math and verbal test scores (on the SAT and ACT). The results indicated significant (but weak) relations between the non-*g* residuals of the shop factor and the math and verbal test scores ($M_\beta \approx -0.12$), indicating that strong

---

3   Preliminary support for SLODR comes from Coyle's [26] study of tilt effects for whites and blacks, two groups that show an average differences in *g* (favoring whites) of about 1 *SD*. In general, tilt levels were higher, and tilt relations with specific abilities were stronger, for whites than for blacks (e.g., [26], p. 32). Such a pattern is consistent with SLODR, which assumes that non-*g* effects (e.g., tilt effects) should be stronger for higher ability groups than for lower ability groups.

non-academic abilities were associated with weak academic abilities. The results suggest a tradeoff in investment in non-academic abilities (shop) and academic abilities (math and verbal), yielding negative effects. Further research is needed to substantiate non-*g* effects with other non-academic abilities (e.g., technical tilt) and to examine whether the effects vary with ability specialization factors (e.g., life history and ability level). In addition, future research could examine other non-academic traits such as social intelligence and Big Five personality traits. Possible candidates include emotional intelligence, agreeableness, and theory of mind, which may predict economic and social criteria (e.g., wealth, trust, prosocial norms) beyond *g* [39].

A *magnification model* summarizes the predictions related to ability specialization and non-*g* factors (Figure 5). The model predicts that non-*g* effects are magnified with increases in ability specialization factors (e.g., life history slowing, educational specialization, ability level). The predictions are depicted in Figure 5, which plots a nonlinear relationship between a non-*g* factor (e.g., ability tilt) and an ability specialization factor. Non-*g* factors (*y*-axis) include ability tilt and non-*g* residuals. Non-*g* effects are assumed to strengthen nonlinearly with ability specialization factors (*x*-axis). The expected increase in non-*g* effects can be formally tested by regressing a non-*g* factor (e.g., tilt level) on the linear and quadratic terms of a specialization factor. A key prediction is that a significant (and positive) quadratic term should account for additional variance beyond the linear term, indicating that non-*g* effects increase nonlinearly as a function of the ability specialization factor.[4]

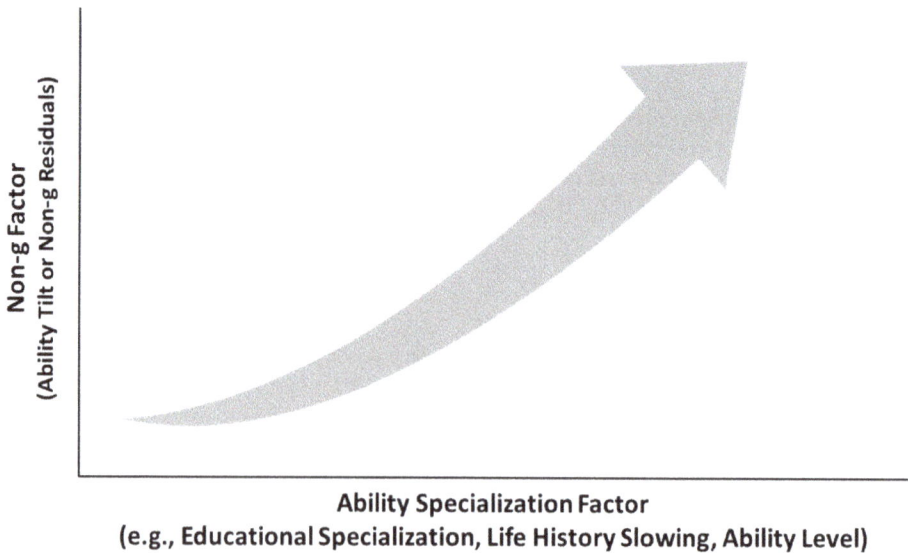

Figure 5. Magnification model of non-*g* factors. Non-*g* effects are predicted to strengthen nonlinearly with ability specialization factors (e.g., ability level, life history, education).

---

[4] The predictions of the magnification model should be tested after correcting for measurement error, which can increase the predictive power of *g* relative to non-*g* factors ([40]; see also, [41]). In addition, corrections for shrinkage should be used to avoid capitalization on chance (e.g., [42], p. 515; see also, [43]), and corrections for range restriction should be used to avoid variance compression, which can reduce effects sizes.

8. Conclusions

The research reviewed here demonstrates the predictive power of non-*g* factors (e.g., ability tilt and non-*g* residuals). In general, non-*g* factors correlate positively with complementary criteria (e.g., math tilt and STEM criteria) and negatively with non-complementary criteria (e.g., math tilt and humanities criteria). The results are consistent with investment theories, which assume that investment in specific abilities (e.g., math/STEM) enhances complementary abilities and inhibits competing abilities (e.g., verbal/humanities). Future research should examine whether non-*g* effects increase with continued investment and ability specialization factors (e.g., life history slowing, ability level, educational specialization).

Acknowledgments: This research was supported by a grant from the National Science Foundation's Interdisciplinary Behavioral and Social Science Research competition (IBSS-L 1620457). Portions of the research were presented at the 2017 conference of the International Society for Intelligence Research. The author thanks the editors of the Special Issue and three anonymous reviewers for their constructive comments.

Conflicts of Interest: The author declares no conflict of interest.

References

1. Coyle, T.R. Relations among general intelligence (*g*) aptitude tests, and GPA: Linear effects dominate. *Intelligence* **2015**, *53*, 16–22. [CrossRef]
2. Frey, M.C.; Detterman, D.K. Scholastic assessment or *g*? The relationship between the scholastic assessment test and general cognitive ability. *Psychol. Sci.* **2004**, *15*, 373–378. [CrossRef] [PubMed]
3. Koenig, K.A.; Frey, M.C.; Detterman, D.K. ACT and general cognitive ability. *Intelligence* **2008**, *36*, 153–160. [CrossRef]
4. Coyle, T.R. Predictive validity of non-*g* residuals of tests: More than *g*. *J. Intell.* **2014**, *2*, 21–25. [CrossRef]
5. Reeve, C.L.; Charles, J.E. Survey of opinions on the primacy of *g* and social consequences of ability testing: A comparison of expert and non-expert views. *Intelligence* **2008**, *36*, 681–688. [CrossRef]
6. Coyle, T.R.; Pillow, D.R. SAT and ACT predict college GPA after removing *g*. *Intelligence* **2008**, *36*, 719–729. [CrossRef]
7. Jensen, A.R. *The g Factor: The Science of Mental Ability*; Praeger: Westport, CT, USA, 1998.
8. Roth, B.; Becker, N.; Romeyke, S.; Schäfer, S.; Domnick, F.; Spinath, F.M. Intelligence and school grades: A meta-analysis. *Intelligence* **2015**, *53*, 118–137. [CrossRef]
9. Schmidt, F.L.; Hunter, J.E. The validity and utility of selection methods in personnel psychology: Practical and theoretical implications of 85 years of research findings. *Psychol. Bull.* **1998**, *124*, 262–274. [CrossRef]
10. Thorndike, R.L. *Intelligence and Information Processing: The Mind and the Computer*; Center on Evaluation, Development, and Research: Bloomington, IN, USA, 1984.
11. Ree, M.J.; Earles, J.A.; Teachout, M.S. Predicting job performance: Not much more than *g*. *J. Appl. Psychol.* **1994**, *79*, 518–524. [CrossRef]
12. Peterson, R.A.; Brown, S.P. On the use of beta coefficients in meta-analysis. *J. Appl. Psychol.* **2005**, *90*, 175–181. [CrossRef] [PubMed]
13. Roth, P.L.; Le, H.; Oh, I.-S.; Van Iddekinge, C.H.; Bobko, P. Using beta coefficients to impute missing correlations in meta-analysis research: Reasons for caution. *J. Appl. Psychol.* **2018**, *103*, 644–658. [CrossRef] [PubMed]
14. Cohen, J. *Statistical Power Analysis for the Behavioral Sciences*, 2nd ed.; Lawrence Erlbaum Associates: Hillsdale, NJ, USA, 1988.
15. Coyle, T.R.; Purcell, J.M.; Snyder, A.C.; Kochunov, P. Non-*g* residuals of the SAT and ACT predict specific abilities. *Intelligence* **2013**, *41*, 114–120. [CrossRef]
16. Cattell, R.B. *Intelligence: Its Structure, Growth and Action*; North-Holland: New York, NY, USA, 1987.
17. Coyle, T.R.; Snyder, A.C.; Richmond, M.C.; Little, M. SAT non-*g* residuals predict course specific GPAs: Support for investment theory. *Intelligence* **2015**, *51*, 57–66. [CrossRef]

18. Lubinski, D. Exceptional cognitive ability: The phenotype. *Behav. Genet.* **2009**, *39*, 350–358. [CrossRef] [PubMed]

19. Achter, J.A.; Lubinski, D.; Benbow, C.P.; Eftekhari-Sanjani, H. Assessing vocational preferences among gifted adolescents adds incremental validity to abilities: A discriminant analysis of educational outcomes over a 10-year interval. *J. Educ. Psychol.* **1999**, *91*, 777–786. [CrossRef]

20. Lubinski, D.; Webb, R.M.; Morelock, M.J.; Benbow, C.P. Top 1 in 10,000: A 10-year follow-up of the profoundly gifted. *J. Appl. Psychol.* **2001**, *86*, 718–729. [CrossRef] [PubMed]

21. Park, G.; Lubinski, D.; Benbow, C.P. Contrasting intellectual patterns predict creativity in the arts and sciences: Tracking intellectually precocious youth over 25 years. *Psychol. Sci.* **2007**, *18*, 948–952. [CrossRef] [PubMed]

22. Wai, J.; Lubinski, D.; Benbow, C.P. Creativity and occupational accomplishments among intellectually precocious youths: An age 13 to age 33 longitudinal study. *J. Educ. Psychol.* **2005**, *97*, 484–492. [CrossRef]

23. Deary, I.J.; Egan, V.; Gibson, G.J.; Brand, C.R.; Austin, E.; Kellaghan, T. Intelligence and the differentiation hypothesis. *Intelligence* **1996**, *23*, 105–132. [CrossRef]

24. Coyle, T.R.; Purcell, J.M.; Snyder, A.C.; Richmond, M.C. Ability tilt on the SAT and ACT predicts specific abilities and college majors. *Intelligence* **2014**, *46*, 18–24. [CrossRef]

25. Coyle, T.R.; Snyder, A.C.; Richmond, M.C. Sex differences in ability tilt: Support for investment theory. *Intelligence* **2015**, *50*, 209–220. [CrossRef]

26. Coyle, T.R. Ability tilt for whites and blacks: Support for differentiation and investment theories. *Intelligence* **2016**, *56*, 28–34. [CrossRef]

27. Coyle, T.R. Non-*g* residuals of group factors predict ability tilt, college majors, and jobs: A non-*g* nexus. *Intelligence* **2018**, *67*, 19–25. [CrossRef]

28. Newton, I. Newton to Hooke. In *The Correspondence of Isaac Newton*; Turnbull, H.W., Ed.; (Original Work Published in 1676); Cambridge University Press: Cambridge, UK, 1959; Volume 1, p. 416.

29. Calvin, D.M.; Fernandes, C.; Smith, P.; Visscher, P.M.; Deary, I.J. Sex, intelligence and educational achievement in a national cohort of over 175,000 11-year-old schoolchildren in England. *Intelligence* **2010**, *38*, 424–432. [CrossRef]

30. Johnson, W.; Bouchard, T.J. Sex differences in mental abilities: *g* masks the dimensions on which they lie. *Intelligence* **2007**, *35*, 23–39. [CrossRef]

31. Wai, J.; Lubinski, D.; Benbow, C.P. Spatial ability for STEM domains: Aligning over 50 years of cumulative psychological knowledge solidifies its importance. *J. Educ. Psychol.* **2009**, *101*, 817–835. [CrossRef]

32. Lewin, K. Problems of research in social psychology. In *Field Theory in Social Science: Selected Theoretical Papers*; Cartwright, D., Ed.; Harper & Row: New York, NY, USA, 1951; pp. 155–169.

33. Spearman, C. *The Abilities of Man: Their Nature and Measurement*; AMS Press: New York, NY, USA, 1932.

34. Blum, D.; Holling, H. Spearman's law of diminishing returns. A meta-analysis. *Intelligence* **2017**, *65*, 60–66. [CrossRef]

35. Woodley, M.A. The cognitive differentiation-integration effort hypothesis: A synthesis between the fitness indicators and life history models of human intelligence. *Rev. Gen. Psychol.* **2011**, *13*, 228–245. [CrossRef]

36. Woodley, M.A.; Figueredo, A.J.; Ross, K.C.; Brown, S.D. Four successful tests of the cognitive differentiation-integration effort hypothesis. *Intelligence* **2013**, *41*, 832–842. [CrossRef]

37. Scarr, S.; McCartney, K. How people make their own environments: A theory of genotype→environment effects. *Child Dev.* **1983**, *54*, 424–435. [PubMed]

38. Bouchard, T.J. Experience producing drive theory: How genes drive experience and shape personality. *Acta Paediatr. Suppl.* **1997**, *422*, 60–64. [CrossRef] [PubMed]

39. Freeman, J.; Coyle, T.R.; Baggio, J.A. The functional intelligences proposition. *Pers. Individ. Differ.* **2016**, *99*, 46–55. [CrossRef]

40. Schmidt, F.L. Beyond questionable research methods: The role of omitted relevant research in the credibility of research. *Arch. Sci. Psychol.* **2017**, *5*, 32–41. [CrossRef]

41. Brown, K.G.; Le, H.; Schmidt, F.L. Specific aptitude theory revisited: Is there incremental validity for training performance? *Int. J. Sel. Assess.* **2006**, *14*, 87–100. [CrossRef]

42. Viswesvaran, C.; Ones, D.S.; Schmidt, F.L.; Le, H.; Oh, I.-S. Measurement error obfuscates scientific knowledge: Path to cumulative knowledge requires corrections for unreliability and psychometric meta-analyses. *Ind. Organ. Psychol. Perspect. Sci. Pract.* **2014**, *7*, 507–518. [CrossRef]
43. Wherry, R.J. A new formula for predicting the shrinkage of the coefficient of multiple correlation. *Ann. Math. Stat.* **1931**, *2*, 440–457. [CrossRef]

Journal of
Intelligence

MDPI

Article

A Tempest in A Ladle: The Debate about the Roles of General and Specific Abilities in Predicting Important Outcomes

Wendy Johnson

Department of Psychology, University of Edinburgh, 7 George Square, Edinburgh EH8 9JZ, UK;
wendy.johnson@ed.ac.uk; Tel.: +44-0131-651-1304

Received: 28 February 2018; Accepted: 12 April 2018; Published: 19 April 2018

Abstract: The debate about the roles of general and specific abilities in predicting important outcomes is a tempest in a ladle because we cannot measure abilities without also measuring skills. Skills always develop through exposure, are specific rather than general, and are executed using different strategies by different people, thus tapping into varied specific abilities. Relative predictive validities of measurement formats depend on the purpose: the more general and long-term the purpose, the better the more general measure. The more specific and immediate the purpose, the better the closely related specific measure.

Keywords: general cognitive ability; specific cognitive abilities; academic achievement; job performance; occupational attainment; health; longevity; situational specificity

---

Excitabat enim fluctus in simpulo ut dicitur Gratidius.

For Gratidius raised a tempest in a ladle.

—Cicero, First century BCE, *De Legisbus*

In 2009, the *Journal of Research in Personality* published a Special Issue assessing the past and future of the famous person-situation debate in personality psychology. The issue, incorporating 81 personality psychologists as authors, included the usual editorial introduction, 38 empirical studies and evaluative essays, and a concluding perspective by Walter Mischel, whose 1968 book [1] is often considered to have originated the debate. One of the essays stood out as having assessed the question's status most clearly, at least for me. It was the single-pager by Robert Hogan [2], who offered four reasons why the debate is 'much ado about nothing'. His bottom line was that no one knows how to measure situations and everyone agrees that what a situation even 'is' depends on the perceptions of the people in them. However, these perceptions are always functions of those people's personalities, so any situation definition would be affected by the very factors 'theory' says they influence.

I perceive the 'situation' of debate about the roles of general and specific abilities in predicting important outcomes to be a similar waste of time and resources. Of course this may be just an expression of my cranky personality—you can be the judge of that after I outline my reasons. Like Hogan's, they do not constitute any kind of formal review, nor are they based on having run all the statistical tests that could be run. They are based, though, on reading a large share of the relevant research, doing many relevant statistical tests, and thinking hard about what we have done, what we can do with what we have, what might be missing, and what we could do to remedy that. At minimum, it is thus a dust-bowl empirically-based abstraction of an abstraction, and maybe a layer or two up from that.

There is massive confusion throughout the cognitive abilities research literature and assessment communities over which tasks measure skills and which measure abilities. I use 'skill' here to refer to performance clearly acquired through exposure and practice, and 'ability' to refer to some inherent capacity to acquire skills in general or particular kinds of skills, a distinction much easier to postulate than to articulate either conceptually or empirically with any clarity. This confusion is understandable because, much as we would like to, we have no assessments that measure purely either ability or skill, probably because there are no, and never could be, such tasks. All purported ability measures, especially those most often claimed otherwise such as the Raven, as evidenced by their large Flynn Effects, tap exposure and practice too, as can be seen by the substantial practice effects that show up just by administering the same test twice, as well as responses to task training. All purported skill measures such as typing or arithmetic tests also tap ability because even when exposure and opportunity to practice are closely controlled, individual differences in performance emerge. However, the primary reason there probably never could be such tasks is that babies can do almost nothing we recognize as cognitive—everything of that sort emerges through exposure and experience during 'development'. It is not just a matter of someday identifying the relevant raw 'biological' material either: the brain is actively sculpted by experience, and genes all have environmentally mediated reaction norms.

Importantly, individual cognitive differences are often strategy-related, e.g., [3,4]. That is, people differ in the ways they do the same tasks, with some strategies being more effective than others. Part of any concept of general ability is the ability to figure out effective and efficient ways of approaching new tasks, so these differences do reflect this general ability. General ability is more than this, though: even when people are taught or told to use specific strategies and given the opportunity to practice before being tested, individual differences in performance remain [5]. This likely indicates differences in some kind of overall implementation capacity, but also indicates differences in which strategies 'come easiest' or 'work best', reflecting differences in what would be considered more specific abilities, as well as differences in prior exposure to relevant material.

The editors' call for articles for this Special Issue of the *Journal of Intelligence* on what they term 'the great debate' about the relative merits of general and specific abilities in predicting real-world outcomes premised the debate on a consensus among researchers and practitioners that the 'structure' of human cognitive abilities can be modeled as a hierarchy consisting of a general ability factor that is associated with various levels of increasingly specific, more narrowly construed abilities. They noted appropriately, however, that this is about as far as any 'consensus' goes. Opinions differ as to just how the various 'levels' are related to each other, just what they might mean 'biologically', and how best to study them. In addition, every time anyone constructs a hierarchical model in a new battery, it comes out looking different from any one that the same person constructed in any other battery, not to mention different from the model some other researcher would construct in that same battery in that same sample. This is because the underlying factor-analytically-based methods are inherently subjective and because the relative associations among specific cognitive tasks vary both with sample specifics and with the specific other cognitive tasks in any battery.

Carroll [6] offered what I hope is the ultimate example of this variation. Try as he might across more than 460 datasets, he could not clearly carve out the natural 'joints' among specific abilities, nor even how many 'levels' of them there might be. My own work with the VPR model [7–11] shows this too: the specifics of the VPR model in each battery were different from every other one. This does not undermine the point of all that work, which was not to be specific about defining VPR model factors or specific abilities—the various verbal–perceptual and fluid-crystallized models all showed analogous differences. Rather, the point was to compare those two modeling perspectives and thus the relevance of their underlying structural premises. There, results were highly consistent, with the VPR model always fitting better. However, neither model 'carved nature at its joints' in any battery any better than Carroll had. This is because factor analysis spits back at us only what we put into it, and we have no tasks that uniquely measure any one particular ability or skill (see above).

At the same time, there is no question that we can design tasks that assess relatively specific, more narrowly construed abilities/skills. There is also no question that, if we have a good broad range of these, we can build yet another hierarchical model, extract its *g* factor in some nice broad sample, and this *g* factor will predict all kinds of important life outcomes from academic achievement to occupational attainment to longevity. Our model will also have a number of more specific factors, and none of them alone will 'outshine' the *g* factor in predicting life outcomes, as long as we keep those life outcomes rather broad. However, if we make the outcomes rather specific, and especially if we make them rather immediate, then those more specific abilities will predict the outcomes too, even after controlling the *g* factor, to the extent that the outcomes have content related to the assessed tasks and the outcomes are soon. Schmidt, Hunter, and Caplan [12] noted long ago that we had better also adjust for measurement error in all factors. Of course they were right, because we want to know about the predictive powers of whatever abilities/skills we are measuring, not those of the scores on whatever tasks we happened to dream up to assess them; so we do that too, and the more specific factors will still predict the outcomes, to the extent noted.

The bottom line for outcome predictors and selection practitioners is straightforward: if you want to predict a rather specific outcome happening rather soon, such as next year's school grades in a specific subject, or seek an employee who can perform productively tomorrow or at least this week, assess specific content/job-related tasks. However, if you are going for long-term prediction and, on the job, are prepared to invest in training and offer incentives that will be needed to keep the employee around to make good on that investment, go for general cognitive ability. For your purposes, you can leave the question of to what degree you just assessed accrued cognitive skills and/or some kind of inherent capacity to the researchers. That one is rather thorny and inevitably developmental rather than merely structural, but the debate over the relative importance of general and specific abilities in predicting important life outcomes is a tempest in a ladle that has run its course.

Conflicts of Interest: The author declares no conflict of interest.

References

1. Mischel, W. *Personality and Assessment*; Wiley: New York, NY, USA, 1968.
2. Hogan, R. Much ado about nothing: The person-situation debate. *J. Res. Persnal.* **2009**, *43*, 249. [CrossRef]
3. Gonthier, C.; Thomassin, N. Strategy use fully mediated the relationship between working memory capacity and performance on Raven's Matrices. *J. Exp. Psychol. Gen.* **2015**, *144*, 916–924. [CrossRef] [PubMed]
4. Lotz, C.; Scherer, R.; Greiff, S.; Sparfeldt, J.R. Intelligence in action—Effective strategy behaviors while solving complex problems. *Intelligence* **2017**, *64*, 98–112. [CrossRef]
5. Hunt, E. Mechanics of verbal ability. *Psychol. Rev.* **1978**, *85*, 109–130. [CrossRef]
6. Carroll, J.B. *Human Cognitive Abilities: A Survey of Factor-Analytic Studies*; CambridgeUniversity Press: Cambridge, UK, 1993.
7. Johnson, W.; Bouchard, T.J. The structure of human intelligence: It's verbal, perceptual, and image rotation (VPR), not fluid and crystallized. *Intelligence* **2005**, *33*, 393–416. [CrossRef]
8. Johnson, W.; Bouchard, T.J. Constructive replication of the Visual-Perceptual-Image Rotation (VPR) Model in Thurstone's (1941) battery of 60 mental tests. *Intelligence* **2005**, *33*, 417–430. [CrossRef]
9. Johnson, W.; Deary, I.J. Placing inspection time, reaction time, and perceptual speed in the broader context of cognitive ability: The VPR model in the Lothian Birth Cohoty 1936. *Intelligence* **2011**, *39*, 405–417. [CrossRef]
10. Johnson, W.; te Nijenhuis, J.; Bouchard, T.J. Replication of the hierarchical Visual-Perceptual-Image Rotation (VPR) Model in de Wolff and Buiten's (1963) battery of 46 tests of mental ability. *Intelligence* **2007**, *35*, 197–2009. [CrossRef]
11. Major, J.T.; Johnson, W.; Deary, I.J. Comparing models of intelligence in Project Talent: The VPR model fits better than the CHC and Extended Gf-Gc Models. *Intelligence* **2012**, *40*, 543–559. [CrossRef]
12. Schmidt, F.L.; Hunter, J.E.; Caplan, J.R. Validity generalization for 2 job groups in the petroleum industry. *J. Appl. Psychol.* **1981**, *66*, 261–273. [CrossRef]

Journal of
Intelligence

MDPI

Commentary

Commenting on the "Great Debate": General Abilities, Specific Abilities, and the Tools of the Trade

Margaret E. Beier [1,*], Harrison J. Kell [2,*] and Jonas W. B. Lang [3,*]

[1] Department of Psychological Sciences, Rice University, Houston, TX 77005, USA
[2] Academic to Career Research Center, Research & Development, Educational Testing Service, Princeton, NJ 08541, USA
[3] Department of Personnel Management, Work, and Organizational Psychology, Ghent University, Henri Dunantlaan 2, 9000 Ghent, Belgium
* Correspondence: beier@rice.edu (M.E.B.); hkell@ets.org (H.J.K.); Jonas.Lang@UGent.be (J.W.B.L.)

Received: 23 January 2019; Accepted: 11 February 2019; Published: 18 February 2019

Abstract: We review papers in the special issue regarding the great debate on general and specific abilities. Papers in the special issue either provided an empirical examination of the debate using a uniform dataset or they provided a debate commentary. Themes that run through the papers and that are discussed further here are that: (1) the importance of general and specific ability predictors will largely depend on the outcome to be predicted, (2) the effectiveness of both general and specific predictors will largely depend on the quality and breadth of how the manifest indicators are measured, and (3) research on general and specific ability predictors is alive and well and more research is warranted. We conclude by providing a review of potentially fruitful areas of future research.

Keywords: cognitive abilities; specific abilities; general abilities; general mental ability; relative importance; narrow abilities; subscores; intelligence; cognitive tests

1. Introduction

Big hammers and long nails are good for securing large items to walls and other large jobs, but they may not be useful in reupholstering a chair. Indeed, a person may be able to attach cloth over the seat of a chair with a large hammer and long nails, but large hammers may damage finished wood and exposed nails may provide unwelcome surprises for sitters. Big tools such as these are useful for their purpose, but not for every purpose. The same is true in the intelligence domain. General ability factors may be useful in predicting broad and complex outcomes, but specific abilities may be more useful determinants when the outcomes are narrower and specific to a content domain. The purpose of the special issue was to engage with the great debate regarding the usefulness of general versus specific ability predictors for an array of outcomes [1].

In the context of industrial and organizational (I-O) psychology (also known as work, organizational, and industrial psychology), the general versus specific abilities debate highlights a pervasive belief about the universal usefulness of the general factor, which seems to be a function of influential papers demonstrating that specific abilities contribute very little to the prediction of job or training performance after a general ability factor (itself derived from these specific factors) is accounted for (e.g., [2–5]). These papers by Ree and colleagues used large samples of military personnel, general and specific predictors derived from the Armed Services Vocational Aptitude Battery (ASVAB), and performance criteria that are collapsed across jobs (i.e., broad performance outcomes). Although one can quibble with the approach that was used by Ree and colleagues, the notion that relevant individual differences in cognitive abilities can fully be captured using a general factor has proven to be problematic for I-O psychology—particularly in the domain of selection and assessment—for a number of reasons. First, legal frameworks in some countries frequently demand that selection occurs using measures that are relevant to the job [6]. In a strict sense, a construct that only consists of a general and universal factor is not suitable for selection in the context of this legal framework [7]. Second, a general factor construct provides very limited insight into how training and development could improve performance. For instance, a company working with pilots may be interested in not only selecting highly able pilots, but also in gaining insight into how the specific limitations of individual pilots can be improved through training. Finally, an issue with a general intelligence factor is that it shows large majority–minority differences that exceed differences for most other constructs (e.g., [8]).

The three unfavorable characteristics of intelligence as a general factor construct have effectively led to a movement in I-O psychology away from intelligence and toward other selection instruments, like assessment centers, situational judgment tests, and interviews [9]. Some of these instruments are also cognitively loaded, however, and may themselves partly measure specific intelligence factors. For example, it has been suggested that verbal and inductive abilities play a role in performance in situational interviews (e.g., [10,11]). In sum, ideas about the universal usefulness of general ability measures have stunted research on the usefulness of specific abilities for predicting work-related outcomes and the development of such measures.

An exception to this trend is found in educational psychology and education more generally. In these fields, many practitioners and policymakers desire to provide students with feedback regarding their strengths and weaknesses in different content areas [12]. One method that many in educational disciplines believe to be a useful means for providing this diagnostic information is the reporting of content-aligned subscores in addition to overall test scores [13]. Indeed, some educational initiatives (e.g., No Child Left Behind) made the provision of diagnostic information a legal requirement, encouraging the use of subscores [14]. However, skepticism remains about the importance of what amounts to specific factors in educational measurement and psychology. The evidence that content-aligned subscores add value that is beyond the total test scores for diagnosis [13–15] and prediction (e.g., [16–18]) is equivocal, and concerns have been expressed related to the psychometric quality of these subscores [19].

The papers in this special issue highlight the arsenal of tools and methods intelligence researchers have at their disposal to best predict performance across contexts and general and specific criteria. Below, we review the excellent papers that were submitted as part of this special issue and provide some directions for future research. To preview the discussion, we conclude that the usefulness of the tool (i.e., general or specific abilities) depends upon the job to be done (i.e., the outcome to be predicted).

2. The Special Issue

In this special issue, authors were invited to write either a) a non-empirical, theoretical, critical, or integrative review on general versus specific abilities for predicting real-world outcomes or b) an empirical analysis of a dataset to answer three questions [1]: Do the data present evidence for the usefulness of specific abilities? How important are specific abilities relative to general abilities for predicting outcomes in the dataset? Also, to what degree could/should researchers use different prediction models for the outcomes in the dataset?

Authors who chose to present an empirical paper were provided with scores on three intelligence tests from a Thurstonian test battery and school grades for German adolescents and young adults ($N = 219$). In perhaps the most straightforward empirical paper examining the contribution of general versus specific abilities for predicting school performance, Wee [20] conducted two analyses (using structural equation modeling [SEM] and a relative-importance analysis) and found that the importance of the general and specific factors depends on the criteria to be predicted. In the SEM, a general ability factor (derived from common variance among predictor ability tests) was the best predictor of a general performance factor (derived from common variance among course grades); the relative importance analysis results were also consistent with this finding. Wee [20] also found that specific abilities were the best predictor of specific course outcomes (e.g., verbal reasoning best predicted

English grades in the relative importance analysis). However, the pattern of results varied across analytical approaches (e.g., verbal reasoning was not predictive of English grades in the SEM analysis after controlling for general ability and general performance). Wee attributes these differences to the diverse ways in which the factors were derived, but the difference in results—which would alter conclusions—provides an important cautionary example of how different methods can be employed to support various theoretical positions in SEM.

Eid, Krumm, Koch, and Schulze [21] use the data that were provided to examine the contribution of general versus specific abilities on student course performance using a latent multiple regression approach that was built on bi-factor models. The description of the process for their analysis and analytic approach suggests that complex bi-factor models can result in large standard errors and difficulty in interpreting solutions (i.e., model identification and convergence problems). They go on to provide alternative approaches for examining questions about the generality of ability; that is, the extended first-order factor model and the bifactor (S-1) model. The contribution of this paper lies in its detailed description of the difficulties of applying complex models to ability data (often comprised of scores that tend to be highly correlated) and the process of trial and error that can sometimes result—even in the context of confirmatory modeling. Concrete recommendations for approaching such analyses are the fruit of their labor from which others can benefit.

Ziegler and Peikert's [22] approach to data analysis was similarly complex, but rather than using various methodological approaches to answer the research questions, these authors take a somewhat novel approach by assessing the changing validity of general versus specific abilities at different levels of complexity of task performance. To test their assumptions, the authors used polynomial regression and found that models containing both linear and non-linear terms outperformed the models with linear terms only—and that this effect was particularly relevant for specific (versus general) abilities. Importantly, they find that the variance that was accounted for by linear and non-linear models differed by content domain (e.g., math, German, English), suggesting that tasks in each of these domains vary in complexity and their ability demands. Unfortunately, researchers have little more than a coarse understanding of task complexity in terms of ability demands at present and this paper serves to remind us of the importance of understanding task demands that are related to criterion performance when selecting predictors.

Although the authors of each of the three empirical papers chose to analyze the data differently, the results of all three articles point to the usefulness of both the general ability factor and specific abilities for predicting educational outcomes. Moreover, the set of papers demonstrates that the results often depend on the analytical approach adopted, a finding that should give pause to many who see modeling as an approach that unequivocally confirms a theoretical position (cf. [23]). The limitations of the individual analytical approaches notwithstanding, the empirical papers highlight the practical importance of using specific ability predictors in educational research, which is related to the design of educational interventions. Indeed, educational practitioners would likely prefer to design interventions that are focused on specific course-related material, as predicted by specific ability tests rather than relying on general ability predictors. The same might be true in the work domain, but to date we know of no research in work psychology (outside of the military context [4]) that links training needs assessment to the type of testing that is done in selection contexts.

The authors of the remaining two papers chose a non-empirical, theoretical, critical, or integrative review to address the debate surrounding general versus specific abilities for predicting real-world outcomes. Coyle's [24] review describes the general versus specific ability debate as the most pressing issue in intelligence research today. This review introduces new ideas regarding the meaning of the residuals that remain after general factors are partialed out of a predictor/criterion relationship (e.g., ability tilt and non-g residuals). Importantly, Coyle also introduces the idea that abilities will change over time through education and experience in ways that might render specific abilities increasingly important as people age (i.e., a magnification model). These ideas align well with theories of skill acquisition and cognitive aging, which highlight the importance of specific abilities (i.e., knowledge and expertise) for success in daily activities (for work and leisure) [25], and investment theories that describe skill and knowledge development as a function of the investment of attentional capacity and reasoning abilities over time [26]. Indeed, given the importance of knowledge and experience for success in daily life for older individuals, it may be that the results of intelligence research using convenience samples of college students and younger will not generalize to older populations. This is unfortunate, as the proportion of older workers continues to grow globally—particularly in industrialized countries [27], and older workers will need to be selected and trained just like younger workers are.

Rather than call it the most important debate in intelligence research, Johnson's [28] review describes the argument about the usefulness of general or specific ability predictors as a "tempest in a ladle" (referencing Hogan [29]). Among the salient points in this review (e.g., that pitting general and specific abilities against each other ignores their dependencies and that the importance of the general versus specific predictors will depend on the outcome), Johnson refutes Spearman's "indifference of the indicator" stance. That is, the idea that general intelligence factors could be derived from any test or set of tests, "provided only that its correlation with *g* is equally high" ([30], p. 197). Johnson reminds readers that general factors are derived from the assessments of specific abilities that are administered (although see [31,32]). She reminds us that if specific ability assessments have certain characteristics, then the general factor will also have these characteristics, and that general factors that are divorced of content do not magically appear out of any set of specific ability assessments. On the contrary, researchers must examine the content of the manifest variables to fully understand the characteristics of the general factors that are derived from them.

3. Ways Forward

In total, the papers in this special edition highlight the importance of different tools—general and specific abilities–for the prediction of an array of performance outcomes in applied settings. They also point to special considerations and cautions for the use of any tool and its accompanying analytical approach. Most salient perhaps is the idea that the value of the predictor will depend on the criterion—that predictors that are aligned with criteria in terms of breadth and content are likely to maximize prediction [33]. Below, we further expand on additional issues in the debate about the usefulness of general versus specific abilities and then describe future research directions for reinvigorating intelligence research in applied psychology.

3.1. Theoretical Status of Specific Abilities

One open question that becomes apparent by comparing the submissions to the special issue is the theoretical nature of specific abilities and how different models define specific abilities in different ways. For example, Wee's [20] contribution alone included two distinct conceptualizations of the relationship between general and specific abilities, with each being aligned with a different analytic strategy. Based upon the contributions to the special issue, along with other approaches in the cognitive abilities literature (e.g., [1–4,34–36]), we can identify at least four distinct theoretical treatments of specific abilities: (1) Indicators of a general factor with the general factor being the source of variance for a proportion of the specific measure (i.e., *g* causes the specific abilities), (2) Orthogonal to *g*, (3) Correlated with the general factor, but without causality specification in either direction, and (4) The source of the general factor, with *g* constituting a formative composite of specific abilities or a phenomenon that emerges from the interaction of specific abilities.

Ree and colleagues' work [2–4] largely takes the perspective that specific abilities are merely indicators of a general factor. By using bi-factor and relative importance approaches, however, several authors in this special issue endorsed the idea that variance that is shared by specific and general abilities does not necessarily always originate with the broader abilities. We suggest that many controversies surrounding the status of specific and general abilities may be resolved by clearly thinking through, and defining a priori, the expected relationships between general and specific abilities prior to conducting data analyses (see also [34–36]).

3.2. Indifference of the Indicator

The principle of the indifference of the indicator, summarized cavalierly in its practical aspect as "for the purpose of indicating the amount of *g* possessed by a person, any test will do just as well as any other", is related to issues regarding the theoretical status of specific abilities ([30], p. 197). We dispute this idea and agree with Johnson's perspective: What you put into a factor analysis largely determines what you get out, so the manifest indicators do matter. A general factor derived from the ASVAB, for example, may look very different from one that is derived from fluid reasoning tests, because individual assessments that comprise the ASVAB rely heavily on knowledge abilities [37].

Contrary to Spearman's classic statement, not only will any test *not* do just as well as any other, it is often challenging to estimate *g* accurately: Using only a small number of tests often leads to poor measurement of *g*, often overestimating its importance [38]. Even when many tests are used, the test content must be sufficiently diverse to fully capture *g*'s generality and not overweight the estimate in terms of one content domain versus another [39]. When *g* estimates are extracted from large test batteries whose scores are modeled using higher-order factor analysis, those scores correlate near-unity, suggesting that they measure the same construct [31,32]. Yet, without careful attention to sample characteristics, score properties, and methodological choices, even when many tests are used to derive *g*, they do not necessarily yield identical results [40]. Adding to the complexity is the fact that, in employment testing situations, it is often not feasible to administer 10 to 20 cognitive tests to derive measures of *g*, which should make investigators cautious about interpreting their results both absolutely and when comparing the value of *g* to that of specific abilities.

The measurement challenges for assessing *g* are only exacerbated when measuring specific abilities. By definition, specific abilities are related to narrower domains than general ability—but multiple tests are still required in order to assess specific abilities with sufficient coverage of the construct. When the number of tests is small, it is likely that researchers are confronted with a considerable level of what some have called specific factor error [41,42]. Specific factor error arises from subjects' idiosyncratic responses to some aspect of the measurement situation (e.g., specific tests to measure a specific ability ability). For specific abilities, the accurate reliability coefficient for detecting this type of error would be a parallel test reliability coefficient between one set of tests and another independent second set of tests to measure the same specific ability. While many studies only use three or fewer indicators/tests for each specific ability, there are some notable exceptions to this rule. For example, Reeve [43] used an average of four tests as indicators of the five specific abilities in his model, Johnson and Deary [44] used an average of six tests across three specific abilities, and Jewsbury, Bowden, and Duff [45] used an average of seven tests across five specific abilities. Indeed, one of the reasons for the poor predictive performance of specific abilities relative to general ability may be that fewer indicators are used to assess them, rendering their estimates less reliable than those of *g* when a specific factor error is taken into account. Further complicating matters is that, just as the dictum of the indifference of the indicator does not always hold for general ability, it does not hold for specific abilities either. Although specific factors are often named in terms of the content of the tests that is used to define them [46], the full breadth of their influence can only be gauged using diverse content to limit specific factor error. For example, a verbal factor derived from tests that are largely composed of synonyms and antonyms will be weighted heavily toward the highly circumscribed content of those assessments; the full comprehensiveness of verbal ability would be better represented by adding sentence completions, reading passages, and vocabulary items. Accurate measurement of general ability is hard—and accurate measurement of specific abilities is even harder.

3.3. Different Levels of Construct Specificity and Cognitive Aging

In the ability domain, decades-old debates about the number and structure of abilities were largely settled by Carroll's [47] reanalysis and derivation of a three-stratum structure of abilities, with *g* (GMA) at its apex, broad abilities comprising the second stratum, and narrow abilities comprising the first stratum (although see Johnson and Bouchard [48] for a competing model). The papers in this special issue have highlighted important differences between general and specific abilities, but they have not specifically addressed the second stratum of broad content abilities (e.g., fluid/reasoning abilities, crystallized/knowledge abilities). Although these broad content abilities are correlated in the population, they have different relationships with other organizationally relevant factors, such as age. Specifically, fluid ability—the ability to reason through novel problems—begins declining in late adolescence/early adulthood and continues its descent throughout the lifespan [26]. By contrast, crystallized abilities—the knowledge that is gained through experience and education—remain stable and can even increase throughout the lifespan [26]. Although age-related ability trajectories will differ across people (e.g., some 50 year olds have the ability profile of 30 year olds while others' more resemble 70 year olds)—perhaps as a consequence of the difficulties of teasing apart knowledge versus reasoning-based strategies at the individual-level (cf. Johnson [28], Johnson & Bouchard [48]) —both longitudinal and cross sectional research demonstrate these normative patterns [49].

In industrialized countries, it is important for I-O practitioners and scientists engaged in testing and selection to be aware of these ability trajectories because, as mentioned earlier, most of the people who are being tested and selected are either approaching or past the age at which fluid abilities begin to decline. The median age in the United States (U.S.) labor force is currently 42 years old and increasing and similar trends can be found globally—at least in similarly industrialized countries [27]. Moreover, many so-called general ability measures are largely derived from fluid ability assessments (e.g., Raven's Progressive Matrices and other abstract reasoning tasks) in an attempt to control for prior exposure in high-stakes assessment situations, such as selection. Because of the age-related changes in abilities described above, such measures will almost certainly put older job applicants at a disadvantage in selection. Crystallized abilities (as assessed by broad cultural knowledge measures) and general knowledge (as assessed by domain knowledge measures) are arguably more important determinants of job performance for many workers whose work engages in relatively routine tasks. However, a significant limitation in the assessment of crystallized/knowledge abilities in selection is a lack of job-relevant measures of knowledge that can be given to job applicants without prior job experience. Although some researchers have doubted that such measures would be useful [50], we encourage researchers to investigate their utility. We consider it extremely likely, for instance, that researchers can identify job-general knowledge that might transfer across many jobs (e.g., developing and managing a budget or project; motivating subordinates; writing a memo or email) that could be assessed in selection contexts in the form of assessment centers, situational judgment tests, or even paper and pencil assessments. Indeed, the need for these types of measures for selection has been highlighted by industrial and organizational psychologists [51], but much research is needed to develop and validate job general domain knowledge measures [52].

3.4. The Effect of Time on Validity Coefficients

The dynamic nature of performance over time is an additional consideration in the general versus specific ability debate that was briefly touched on by Coyle [24] and Johnson [28]. Coyle posited that general ability measures would have their highest validity for predicting early relative to later performance (e.g., [53,54]), calling into question the usefulness of such measures for selection purposes when worker tenure is long [55,56]. The reasons for these declining validities have been the subject of much debate [57–59], but researchers have generally converged on the idea that shifting validities are related to changes in the determinants of the criteria over time, as the task is learned [56].

Coyle's [24] conclusion—that the ability determinants of performance will change as people gain expertise and skill—aligns well with theories of skill acquisition, which state that general ability is an important determinant of performance in early stages of skill acquisition when tasks require processing novel information. At later stages of skill acquisition, however, different abilities become more salient determinants of performance [60,61]. One caveat is that general ability should remain predictive of performance for inconsistent or complex skills—that is, skills that are very difficult or impossible to learn/automate. Research on skill acquisition and skilled performance also shows that the types of abilities that become more salient with skill acquisition and practice are those abilities that are more aligned with the criterion, such psychomotor ability and typing skill and verbal fluency and writing ability. Moreover, it has also been suggested that specific abilities should be key in acquiring specific types of job knowledge, while general abilities should be key in acquiring general varieties of job knowledge [62]. The consideration of time highlights the idea that both general and specific abilities may be great tools for predicting performance—but at different points in time (general ability earlier—specific abilities later).

Most of the research that was conducted to examine the idea that different abilities will be the best predictors of performance at different stages of skill acquisition has been conducted in laboratory settings using relatively circumscribed tasks (such as skill acquisition on an air traffic control task; [60]). One exception is a longitudinal study that found that general ability was the most predictive of job performance at early stages of a job, but more specific abilities (i.e., psychomotor ability) became more predictive of job performance later, provided that job tasks were consistent. Conversely, general ability remained an important predictor over time for more complex (inconsistent) jobs [63]. With the exception of this study [63], the over-reliance on research that uses relatively short periods of time (e.g., cross sectional studies) may have biased findings in the literature systematically against detecting the effects of specific abilities. More longitudinal research is needed.

Johnson [28] also touched on the role of time when considering the relative applied value of measures of general versus specific cognitive abilities, noting that specific measures are preferable when criterion measurement takes place soon after assessment scores are gathered and vice-versa for general measures (and especially when the breadth of the criterion is matched with that of the predictor). This claim appears to contradict Coyle's [24], but it was couched in terms that are more general than job performance, including long-term life outcomes, such as occupational attainment and longevity. Over very long periods of time, not only might the ability determinants of task performance change, so might the tasks themselves (e.g., long-tenured employees in the same organization may have very different job duties 20 years after being hired). As noted earlier, when the nature of the criterion (and its underlying constituents) is complex or obscure and the timespan for its assessment indeterminate, the broad hammer of a general ability measure may be preferable to the surgeon's scalpel of a specific one.

3.5. The Criterion Problem

Above, we have made the case that the effectiveness of either general or specific ability measures for predicting performance is largely a function of what one is trying to predict (i.e., the criterion). Unfortunately, in many applied areas of research—and particularly in work psychology—the criterion is often neither well defined nor well measured [64]. We suspect that some of the debate regarding the usefulness of general versus specific abilities on the predictor side, including what we consider to be a premature conclusion that general ability is always the most effective predictor of performance, is a function of the coarseness of criterion measures. Because the criteria are relatively vague and ill defined, the use of general ability measures helps to ensure that at least some variance in the criterion will be accounted for, even though we may know relatively little about the criterion construct (e.g., whether it is uni- or multi-dimensional). To revive our earlier metaphor, if we cannot see what we are hitting, the biggest hammer is more likely than the smaller hammer to hit at least something! Similarly, the "not much more than *g*" approach [2–4] may be a good first swing at predicting a coarse outcome, but more precision in predictor and criterion measurement would better serve our science.

Indeed, the multidimensional nature of performance has been known for a long time, as Toops said in 1944 "Even in simple jobs success is multidimensional" ([65], p. 274). Just because we do not measure them well, does not mean that these multidimensional facets of performance do not exist. It has been 25 years since Austin and Villanova published their seminal review of the criterion problem in I-O psychology. In that paper, they decried the lack of attention on the criterion side, particularly as compared to the intense focus on predictors (see Schmidt & Hunter [50]), among others). In the intervening two and a half decades, researchers have made small steps in recognizing two dimensions of job performance: Task performance (behavior supports the technical core) and contextual performance (behavior that contributes to the context in which work gets done [66]). Although an improvement, these dimensions continue to be relatively broad. An exception to this rule is arguably Campbell's work on the U.S. Army's Project A [67,68]. Campbell established relatively well defined specific job performance dimensions that were relevant to the set of jobs in the Army being studied. Re-analyses of the Project A validity data (see Kell & Lang [69] for an overview) actually supports the notion that specific abilities are related to specific criteria and they provide a window into how future work could link specific abilities to specific criteria. We hope that this special issue will serve to both revive interest in general and specific ability predictors and interest in better defining performance criteria.

4. Conclusions

This special issue brought a diverse group of scholars together. We thank all of the participating author teams for their excellent papers and our reviewers for their insight and helpful and constructive comments. In our initial call for this special issue, we provided a typical educational dataset and asked potential contributors three questions: Do the data present evidence for the usefulness of specific abilities? How important are specific abilities relative to general abilities for predicting outcomes in the dataset? Also, to what degree could/should researchers use different prediction models for the outcomes in the dataset? Our hope in starting with a typical dataset was to gain diverse and new insights beyond the general notion that there is "not much more than *g*" when it comes to linking intelligence to outcome criteria. Most researchers and practitioners working with intelligence measures face similar questions and datasets. As we noted in the introduction to this comment, there has long been a notion in the intelligence literature that the answer to all three questions is clearly: No, not important, and different prediction models are unnecessary. As we suggested above, the focus on *g* in the applied intelligence literature has potentially long hampered progress and innovation in the field. The three empirical papers and two commentaries provide a set of novel perspectives and ideas that are new to us. The contributions show that research on general and specific abilities is alive and well, and describe how a focus on specific abilities can help researchers and practitioners gain valuable additional insights into the determinants of performance over general abilities. The contributions also demonstrate how researchers can simultaneously consider general and specific measures in their research and balance and reconcile the opposing viewpoints on their potential benefits. We believe that these ideas provide a building block for more balanced and informed perspectives on the role of general and specific abilities and future progress in applied research on intelligence.

Author Contributions: Writing-original draft preparation, M.E.B.; writing—review revision, and editing, M.E.B., H.J.K., J.W.B.L.

Funding: This research received no external funding.

Conflicts of Interest: The authors declare no conflict of interest.

References

1. Kell, H.J.; Lang, J.W.B. The great debate: General ability and specific abilities in the prediction of important outcomes. *J. Intell.* **2018**, *6*, 39. [CrossRef]
2. Ree, M.J.; Carretta, T.R.; Teachout, M.S. Pervasiveness of dominant general factors in organizational measurement. *Ind. Organ. Psychol.* **2015**, *8*, 409–427. [CrossRef]
3. Ree, M.J.; Earles, J.A. Predicting training success: Not much more than *g*. *Pers. Psychol.* **1991**, *44*, 321–332. [CrossRef]
4. Ree, M.J.; Earles, J.A.; Teachout, M.S. Predicting job performance: Not much more than *g*. *J. Appl. Psychol.* **1994**, *79*, 518–524. [CrossRef]

5. Hunter, J.E. A causal model of cognitive ability, job knowledge, job performance, and supervisor ratings. In *Performance Measurement and Theory*; Landy, F.J., Zedeck, S., Cleveland, J., Eds.; Lawrence Erlbaum Associates: Hillsdale, NJ, USA, 1983; pp. 257–266.

6. Outtz, J.L. The role of cognitive ability tests in employment selection. *Hum. Perform.* **2002**, *15*, 161–171.

7. Landy, F.J. Validity generalization: Then and now. In *Validity Generalization: A Critical Review*; Murphy, K.R., Ed.; Lawrence Erlbaum Associates: Hillsdale, NJ, USA, 2003; pp. 155–195.

8. Hough, L.M.; Oswald, F.L. Personnel selection: Looking toward the future–Remembering the past. *Ann. Rev. Psychol.* **2000**, *51*, 631–664. [CrossRef] [PubMed]

9. Scherbaum, C.A.; Goldstein, H.W.; Yusko, K.P.; Ryan, R.; Hanges, P.J. Intelligence 2.0: Reestablishing a research program on g in I–O psychology. *Ind. Organ. Psychol.* **2012**, *5*, 128–148. [CrossRef]

10. Huffcutt, A.I.; Roth, P.L. Racial group differences in employment interview evaluations. *J. Appl. Psychol.* **1998**, *83*, 179–189. [CrossRef]

11. Janz, T. The patterned behavior description interview: The best prophet of future is the past. In *The Employment Interview: Theory, Research, and Practice*; Eder, R.W., Ferris, G.R., Eds.; Sage: Newbury Park, CA, USA, 1989; pp. 158–168.

12. Meijer, R.R.; Boévé, A.J.; Tendeiro, J.N.; Bosker, R.J.; Albers, C.J. The use of subscores in higher education: When is this useful? *Front. Psychol.* **2017**, *8*, 305. [CrossRef]

13. Liu, R.; Qian, H.; Luo, X.; Woo, A. Relative diagnostic profile: A subscore reporting framework. *Educ. Psychol. Meas.* **2017**, *78*, 1072–1088. [CrossRef]

14. Sinharay, S. How often do subscores have added value? Results from operational and simulated data. *J. Educ. Meas.* **2010**, *47*, 150–174. [CrossRef]

15. Sinharay, S.; Puhan, G.; Haberman, S.J. An NCME instructional module on subscores. *Educ. Meas.* **2011**, *30*, 29–40. [CrossRef]

16. Glutting, J.J.; Watkins, M.W.; Konold, T.R.; McDermott, P.A. Distinctions without a difference: The utility of observed versus latent factors from the WISC-IV in estimating reading and math achievement on the WIAT-II. *J. Spec. Educ.* **2006**, *40*, 103–114. [CrossRef]

17. Kahana, S.Y.; Youngstrom, E.A.; Glutting, J.J. Factor and subtest discrepancies on the differential ability scales: Examining prevalence and validity in predicting academic achievement. *Assessment* **2002**, *9*, 82–93. [CrossRef] [PubMed]

18. Youngstrom, E.A.; Kogos, J.L.; Glutting, J.J. Incremental efficacy of Differential Ability Scales factor scores in predicting individual achievement criteria. *Sch. Psychol. Q.* **1999**, *14*, 26–39. [CrossRef]

19. Haberman, S.J. When can subscores have value? *J. Educ. Behav. Stat.* **2008**, *33*, 204–229. [CrossRef]

20. Wee, S. Aligning predictor-criterion bandwidths: Specific abilities as predictors of specific performance. *J. Intell.* **2018**, *6*, 40. [CrossRef]

21. Eid, M.; Krumm, S.; Koch, T.; Schulze, J. Bifactor models for predicting criteria by general and specific factors: Problems of nonidentifiability and alternative solutions. *J. Intell.* **2018**, *6*, 42. [CrossRef]

22. Ziegler, M.; Peikert, A. How specific abilities might throw 'g' a curve: An idea on how to capitalize on the predictive validity of specific cognitive abilities. *J. Intell.* **2018**, *6*, 41. [CrossRef]

23. Tomarken, A.J.; Waller, N.G. Potential problems with "well fitting" models. *J. Abnorm. Psychol.* **2003**, *112*, 578–598. [CrossRef] [PubMed]

24. Coyle, T. Non-g factors predict educational and occupational criteria: More than g. *J. Intell.* **2018**, *6*, 43. [CrossRef]

25. Ackerman, P.L. Adult intelligence: The construct and the criterion problem. *Perspect. Psychol. Sci.* **2017**, *12*, 987–998. [CrossRef] [PubMed]

26. Cattell, R.B. *Intelligence: Its Structure, Growth, and Action*; Elsevier Science: New York, NY, USA, 1987.

27. Toossi, M. Labor Force Projections to 2022: The Labor Force Participation Rate Continues to fall. In *Monthly Labor Review*; 4 May 2015; U.S. Bureau of Labor Statistics: Washington, DC, USA, December 2013. Available online: http://www.bls.gov/opub/mlr/2013/article/labor-force-projections-to-2022-the-labor-force-participation-rate-continues-to-fall.htm (accessed on 13 February 2019).

28. Johnson, W. A tempest in a ladle: The debate about the roles of general and specific abilities in predicting important outcomes. *J. Intell.* **2018**, *6*, 24. [CrossRef]

29. Hogan, R. Much ado about nothing: The person–situation debate. *J. Res. Personal.* **2009**, *43*, 249. [CrossRef]

30. Spearman, C. *The Abilities of Man*; Macmillan: New York, NY, USA, 1927.

31. Johnson, W.; Bouchard, T.J., Jr.; Krueger, R.F.; McGue, M.; Gottesman, I.I. Just one *g*: Consistent results from three test batteries. *Intelligence* **2004**, *32*, 95–107. [CrossRef]

32. Johnson, W.; te Nijenhuis, J.; Bouchard, T.J., Jr. Still just 1 *g*: Consistent results from five test batteries. *Intelligence* **2008**, *36*, 81–95. [CrossRef]

33. Wittmann, W.W.; Süß, H.-M. Investigating the paths between working memory, intelligence, knowledge, and complex problem-solving performances via Brunswik symmetry. In *Learning and Individual Differences: Process, Trait, and Content Determinants*; Ackerman, P.L., Kyllonen, P.C., Roberts, R.D., Eds.; American Psychological Association: Washington, DC, USA, 1999; pp. 77–108.

34. Lang, J.W.B.; Kersting, M.; Hülsheger, U.R.; Lang, J. General mental ability, narrower cognitive abilities, and job performance: The perspective of the nested-factors model of cognitive abilities. *Pers. Psychol.* **2010**, *63*, 595–640. [CrossRef]

35. Lang, J.W.B.; Bliese, P.D. I–O psychology and progressive research programs on intelligence. *Ind. Organ. Psychol.* **2012**, *5*, 161–166. [CrossRef]

36. Stanhope, D.S.; Surface, E.A. Examining the incremental validity and relative importance of specific cognitive abilities in a training context. *J. Pers. Psychol.* **2014**, *13*, 146–156. [CrossRef]

37. Roberts, R.D.; Goff, G.N.; Anjoul, F.; Kyllonen, P.C.; Pallier, G.; Stankov, L. The Armed Services Vocational Aptitude Battery (ASVAB): Little more than acculturated learning (Gc)!? *Learn. Individ. Differ.* **2000**, *12*, 81–103. [CrossRef]

38. Major, J.T.; Johnson, W.; Bouchard, T.J., Jr. The dependability of the general factor of intelligence: Why small, single-factor models do not adequately represent *g*. *Intelligence* **2011**, *39*, 418–433. [CrossRef]

39. Lohman, D.F.; Lakin, J.M. Intelligence and reasoning. In *The Cambridge Handbook of Intelligence*; Sternberg, R.J., Kaufman, S.B., Eds.; Cambridge University Press: New York, NY, USA, 2011; pp. 419–441.

40. Floyd, R.G.; Clark, M.H.; Shadish, W.R. The exchangeability of IQs: Implications for professional psychology. *Prof. Psychol.* **2008**, *39*, 414–423. [CrossRef]

41. Nunnally, J.C.; Bernstein, I.H. *Psychometric Theory*, 3rd ed.; McGraw-Hill: New York, NY, USA, 1994.

42. Schmidt, F.L.; Le, H.; Ilies, R. Beyond alpha: An empirical examination of the effects of different sources of measurement error on reliability estimates for measures of individual-differences constructs. *Psychol. Methods* **2003**, *8*, 206–224. [CrossRef] [PubMed]

43. Reeve, C.L. Differential ability antecedents of general and specific dimensions of declarative knowledge: More than *g*. *Intelligence* **2004**, *32*, 621–652. [CrossRef]

44. Johnson, W.; Deary, I.J. Placing inspection time, reaction time, and perceptual speed in the broader context of cognitive ability: The VPR model in the Lothian Birth Cohort 1936. *Intelligence* **2011**, *39*, 405–417. [CrossRef]

45. Jewsbury, P.A.; Bowden, S.C.; Duff, K. The Cattell–Horn–Carroll model of cognition for clinical assessment. *J. Psychoeduc. Assess.* **2017**, *35*, 547–567. [CrossRef]

46. Steiger, J.H. Factor indeterminacy in the 1930's and the 1970's some interesting parallels. *Psychometrika* **1979**, *44*, 157–167. [CrossRef]

47. Carroll, J.B. *Human Cognitive Abilities: A Survey of Factor-Analytic Studies*; Cambridge University Press: Cambridge, UK, 1993.

48. Johnson, W.; Bouchard, T.J. The structure of human intelligence: It is verbal, perceptual, and image rotation (VPR), not fluid and crystallized. *Intelligence* **2005**, *33*, 393–416. [CrossRef]

49. Schaie, K.W. *Developmental Influences on Adult Intelligence: The Seattle Longitudinal Study*, 2nd ed.; Oxford University Press: New York, NY, USA, 2013.

50. Schmidt, F.L.; Hunter, J.E. The validity and utility of selection methods in personnel psychology: Practical and theoretical implications of 85 years of research findings. *Psychol. Bull.* **1998**, *124*, 262–274. [CrossRef]

51. Ryan, A.M.; Ployhart, R.E. A century of selection. *Annu. Rev. Psychol.* **2014**, *65*, 693–717. [CrossRef]

52. Beier, M.E.; Young, C.K.; Villado, A.J. Job knowledge: Its definition, development and measurement. In *The SAGE Handbook of Industrial, Work and Organizational Psychology: Personnel Psychology and Employee Performance*, 2nd ed.; SAGE Publications Ltd.: Los Angeles, CA, USA, 2018; Volume 3, pp. 279–298.

53. Lin, P.; Humphreys, L.G. Predictions of academic performance in graduate and professional school. *Appl. Psychol. Meas.* **1977**, *1*, 249–257. [CrossRef]

54. Sturman, M.C. The past, present, and future of dynamic performance research. In *Research in Personnel and Human Resources Management*; Martocchio, J.J., Ed.; Emerald Group Publishing Limited: Bingley, UK, 2007; Volume 26, pp. 49–110.

55. Beier, M.E.; Ackerman, P.L. Time in personnel selection. In *The Oxford Handbook of Personnel Selection and Assessment*; Schmitt, N., Ed.; Oxford University Press: New York, NY, USA, 2012; pp. 721–739.

56. Dahlke, J.A.; Kostal, J.W.; Sackett, P.R.; Kuncel, N.R. Changing abilities vs. changing tasks: Examining validity degradation with test scores and college performance criteria both assessed longitudinally. *J. Appl. Psychol.* **2018**, *103*, 980–1000. [CrossRef] [PubMed]

57. Ackerman, P.L. Within-task intercorrelations of skilled performance: Implications for predicting individual differences? A comment on Henry & Hulin, 1987. *J. Appl. Psychol.* **1989**, *74*, 360–364.

58. Barrett, G.V.; Alexander, R.A.; Doverspike, D. The implications for personnel selection of apparent declines in predictive validities over time: A critique of Hulin, Henry, and Noon. *Pers. Psychol.* **1992**, *45*, 601–617. [CrossRef]

59. Hulin, C.L.; Henry, R.A.; Noon, S.L. Adding a dimension: Time as a factor in the generalizability of predictive relationships. *Psychol. Bull.* **1990**, *107*, 328–340. [CrossRef]

60. Ackerman, P.L. Individual differences in skill learning: An integration of psychometric and information processing perspectives. *Psychol. Bull.* **1987**, *102*, 3–27. [CrossRef]

61. Anderson, J.R. Acquisition of cognitive skill. *Psychol. Rev.* **1982**, *89*, 369–406. [CrossRef]

62. Schneider, W.J.; Newman, D.A. Intelligence is multidimensional: Theoretical review and implications of specific cognitive abilities. *Hum. Resour. Manag. Rev.* **2015**, *25*, 12–27. [CrossRef]

63. Farrell, J.N.; McDaniel, M.A. The stability of validity coefficients over time: Ackerman's (1988) model and the General Aptitude Test Battery. *J. Appl. Psychol.* **2001**, *86*, 60–79. [CrossRef] [PubMed]

64. Austin, J.T.; Villanova, P. The criterion problem: 1917–1992. *J. Appl. Psychol.* **1992**, *77*, 836–874. [CrossRef]

65. Toops, H.A. The criterion. *Educ. Psychol. Meas.* **1994**, *4*, 271–297. [CrossRef]

66. Borman, W.C.; Motowidlo, S.J. Expanding the criterion domain to include elements of contextual performance. In *Personnel Selection in Organizations*; Schmitt, N., Borman, W.C., Eds.; Jossey-Bass: San Francisco, CA, USA, 1993; pp. 71–98.

67. Campbell, J.P.; McHenry, J.J.; Wise, L.L. Modeling job performance in a population of jobs. *Pers. Psychol.* **1990**, *43*, 313–575. [CrossRef]

68. McHenry, J.J.; Hough, L.M.; Toquam, J.L.; Hanson, M.A.; Ashworth, S. Project A validity results: The relationship between predictor and criterion domains. *Pers. Psychol.* **1990**, *43*, 335–354. [CrossRef]

69. Kell, H.J.; Lang, J.W.B. Specific abilities in the workplace: More important than *g*? *J. Intell.* **2017**, *5*, 13. [CrossRef]

MDPI
St. Alban-Anlage 66
4052 Basel
Switzerland
Tel. +41 61 683 77 34
Fax +41 61 302 89 18
www.mdpi.com

Journal of Intelligence Editorial Office
E-mail: jintelligence@mdpi.com
www.mdpi.com/journal/jintelligence

www.ingramcontent.com/pod-product-compliance
Lightning Source LLC
Chambersburg PA
CBHW051316020426
42333CB00028B/3370